OPERATIONS MANUAL

SIEGE WARFARE

First published in March 2018

A catalogue record for this book is available from the British Library.

ISBN 978 1 78521 146 1

Library of Congress control no. 2017948598

Published by Haynes Publishing,
Sparkford, Yeovil, Somerset BA22 7JJ, UK.
Tel: 01963 440635
Int. tel: +44 1963 440635
Website: www.haynes.com

Haynes North America Inc.,
859 Lawrence Drive, Newbury Park,
California 91320, USA.

Printed in Malaysia.

Author's note

Images are credited in captions. Thanks to Alamy and Getty for permission to use their images in this book, unmarked images are from Shutterstock, images marked Cadw are reproduced with the kind permission of the Cadw Photographic Library (Welsh Castles) © Crown Copyright (2017). When photographs have been sourced under Creative Commons licences, the licence is listed in the photo credit. 'PD' is given for Public Domain images.

OPERATIONS MANUAL
SIEGE WARFARE

Dr Chris McNab

From ancient times to the beginning of the gunpowder age

CONTENTS

1 SETTING THE SIEGE

4 HIGH-TRAJECTORY FIRE: THE AGE OF THE TREBUCHET

5 UNDER AND OVER: SIEGE TOWERS AND ESCALADE

2 BRUTE FORCE: BATTERING RAMS AND BORERS

3 BOLTS AND BOULDERS: CATAPULT AND TORSION ENGINES

6 DARK ARTS: SUBTERFUGE, SABOTAGE AND DIPLOMACY

7 FIREPOWER: INCENDIARY AND GUNPOWDER WEAPONS

INTRODUCTION

The essence of war is a violent struggle between two hostile, independent and irreconcilable wills, each trying to impose itself on the other. War is fundamentally an interactive social process. Clausewitz called it a *zweikampf* (literally a 'two-struggle') and suggested the image of a pair of wrestlers locked in a hold, each exerting force and counterforce to try to throw the other. War is thus a process of continuous mutual adaptation, of give and take, move and countermove.

– US Marine Corps, *Warfighting*, 1997

The opening quotation above, from the US Marine Corps' influential *Warfighting* manual, does not relate specifically to the practice of siege warfare, but it perfectly encapsulates it. The 'irreconcilable wills', in the case of siege warfare, are the besieging army and the besieged, both struggling to gain dominance over the other by a 'process of continual mutual adaptation'. In modern times, the idea of a siege tends to relate to small-scale police sieges relating to hostage situations, or on a larger scale, the rough investment of a city in a conflict zone, such as occurred in Sarajevo in 1992–96. Yet for thousands of years, from the Bronze Age to the Renaissance, sieges largely referred to the complete physical encirclement of a fortress or of a fortified city. The central physical condition of the siege was that there was a literal wall between the besiegers outside and the besieged within.

This book is about how the forces both sides of the wall negotiated this situation, on tactical, practical and technological levels. For, despite the breadth of the period covered in this book, the essential tactics for setting or surviving a siege actually remained remarkably constant. For the besiegers, the overall options were primarily: 1) Achieve a non-violent capitulation through diplomacy or threat; 2) Force submission through the privations imposed by a prolonged blockade; 3) Take the fortification through violent action. On the opposite side, the besiegers hoped for

one of the following outcomes: 1) They capitulate peacefully and are treated respectfully by their opponents; 2) Their endurance outlasts that of the besiegers, who are eventually forced to call it a day and retreat; 3) A relief force comes to their rescue; 4) They defeat all enemy assaults in turn, leading to a straightforward military victory. Because sieges typically took place over extended periods of time, however, the objectives of a siege could shift between all these options for the combatants, producing regular highs and crushing lows. In 1570, for example, the cathedral fort of Ishiyama Honganji in Osaka, Japan, was placed under siege by the forces of the great, belligerent Oda Nobunaga. In 1580, the fortification's resistance finally crumbled, but only after a full decade of attrition and violence, in which the tactical balance swung regularly in favour of one side or the other. Ultimately, it was mainly the wearing effects of time that brought Oda victory.

One of the reason sieges are so fascinating to study is that they demonstrate, in a relatively confined geographical space, tactical measure and countermeasure with great clarity. In many ways, there is far less of the 'fog of war' in siege combat than in open battlefield manoeuvre. One of the key reasons for this is that the besieger has an extremely clear objective in view – the fortress. Yet as we shall see, the 'force and counterforce' of a siege battle meant that the outcome of any siege was rarely certain.

▶ The siege of a castle in the 14th century depicts hand-to-hand fighting on a scaling ladder thrown against the battlements, while the garrison hurl stones from a catapult. (Alamy)

▶ An impressively huge reconstructed ballista in the grounds of Warwick Castle, England. (Kumar Sriskandan/Alamy)

1

SETTING THE SIEGE

Placing a large and well-defended fortification under siege was an immense effort in logistics, perseverance and tactical judgement. At the moment the siege was locked into place, those on both sides of the wall often had little sense whether the battle would last a matter of days, weeks, months or even years.

◄ *This depiction of the siege of the castle of Mortagne, near Bordeaux, in 1377, illustrates both land and naval blockades in force. (Getty)*

FORTRESSES, TACTICS AND LOGISTICS

The outcome of a siege was rarely certain at the outset. Unpredictable and violent factors came continually into play – from weather conditions and the spread of disease through to the applications of siege weaponry and shrewdly timed assault tactics. The two constants for both sides, however, were time and logistics.

THE CHALLENGE – FORTIFICATIONS

Understanding the very nature of siege warfare requires, of necessity, a general insight into fortresses and fortifications. First, we must not let the theme of this book deflect us from the true purpose of fortifications. Their formidable physical structure and typically dominant location was first and foremost about power *projection*, not about an anxious

resistance to the outside world. A major fortress, fortified city or castle was the place from which a king, lord or other ruler controlled the surrounding territories and peoples, his garrison typically being ready to sortie out from the castle against threats foreign and domestic. This is why, in essence, fortifications were rarely just bypassed and forgotten by invading or conquering armies – if they did so, the fortresses would remain a threat to the rear, challenging the army's lines of communication and their control of the surrounding territory. One of the key reasons that William the Conqueror (r. 1066–87) suppressed British resistance so convincingly

▼ *The Field Gate of Caen Castle, protected by a muscular barbican that includes a stone machiolated section set like hoarding above the entrance. (Urban/CC-BY-SA-3.0)*

▶ *The ruins of Hastings Castle, the first fortress built by the invading Normans in England.*

▼ *Krak des Chevaliers in Syria, one of the most imposing fortresses in the world, set atop a 650m (2,130ft) plateau. (Bernard Gagnon/CC).*

was that the British had no developed system of fortification. The Normans, by contrast, brought a tested and developed knowledge of fortress building with them, expressed in such mighty bastions as the Château de Caen, which covered 5.5 hectares (13.6 acres) of land. As part of the Normans' active strategy of conquest, more than 500 castles were built at key strategic locations throughout Britain, each providing an operating base for troops, a centre of local governance and a looming visual deterrent against thoughts of resistance.

The *offensive* properties of the fortification are important to our study because shutting and barring the gates and hunkering down inside were not the only options available to the besieged, who could present a more active defence. Based on the fact that the defenders were typically far fewer in number, or far less militarized, than the attackers (otherwise they would have fought an open battle), the best moment for them to sortie out was when the besiegers were just arriving on the battlefield, and had yet to establish any significant siege lines. This is what the 2,300 Hungarian defenders attempted on 2 August 1566 during the initial day of fighting in the siege of Szigetvár, Hungary, putting a significant dent – although ultimately a futile one – in the ranks of more than 100,000 Turks led by the commander Grand Vizier Sokollu Mehmed Pasha. Even if a fortification could be locked under siege, lightning sorties from a well-trained garrison remained a threat to the besieging forces, particularly if they targeted limited objectives such as small sections of the siege camp or valuable siege engines. At the siege of Acre (1189–91), during

▶ *An elevated view of the siege of Szigetvár castle in the 16th century. Much of the castle was destroyed in a powder magazine explosion.(PD)*

the Crusades, Muslim defenders made several sorties out to destroy ram engines with incendiary devices, much to the chagrin of the outmanoeuvred Western knights.

Although fortifications had undoubted offensive and political purposes, they were obviously built with defence very much in mind, using every advantage of location, layout, construction and weaponry to endure a potentially prolonged siege. Here we must acknowledge that our blanket use of the term 'fortress' covers a vast range of building types, from isolated keeps on a hillock as part of a medieval motte-and-bailey design, to sprawling fortified cities containing multiple defensive lines within the outer walls. Only general outlines are possible here – further details will be added as we work through subsequent chapters of this book.

LOCATION

Location was in many ways the centrepiece of a fortification's defence. At least until the advent of heavy gunpowder artillery, the most advantageous location for a fortification was on high ground, the elevation of the fortress making the job of assaulting it that much harder (it is far easier to defend downhill than fight uphill), while natural contours and features could limit the avenues of approach. The Middle East has some particularly fine surviving examples from its history. The Nimrod Fortress on the southern slopes of Mount Hermon, built by Al-Aziz 'Uthman in 1299 to guard over the Golan Heights, stands on a treacherous ridge rising about 800m (2,600ft) above sea level. Syria has the formidable Krak des Chevaliers, a Crusader castle of enormous scale and

historical importance sitting on a 650m (2,130ft) high outcrop east of Tartus. There are also many precipitous and well-sited examples in the Western world. The famous Alcázar of Segovia, Spain, is a superlative example of a 'ship fortress', so called because the fortress occupies a long slender rocky spur set between the confluence of two rivers, with the steep inclines and the rivers at the base making for an excellent defensive site.

Not every fortification could take advantage of high ground, but other natural features provided some measure of protection. Rivers – just mentioned in the context of Alcázar of Segovia – could be excellent outlying barriers, particularly if wide, deep and fast flowing. Watercourses and lakes could also be diverted to form contrived water barriers. Such is particularly evident in Caerphilly Castle in Wales, the fortress being surrounded by artificial lakes, created by damming local rivers. Other natural defences included marshland, areas covered with thick vegetation and particularly rocky or uneven ground (causing problems for wheel-mounted siege engines). Locating your castle on a slab of thick natural rock also caused problems for enemy attempts at undermining.

One of the most substantial of natural defences was the sea. Many fortresses, particularly those connected to or part of a fortified city, occupied coastal locations, for reasons of access to maritime trade and the consumable riches of the seas. Unless a besieging army was accompanied by a fleet substantial enough to impose a naval blockade as well, the seaward side of a fortress's defences could remain an open and invaluable lifeline, bringing in reinforcements and keeping the garrison and populace supplied. The sea could rarely ensure the survival and endurance of the fortress on an indefinite basis, however. Sooner or later, the besiegers would either impose a naval blockade, or the shipborne supplies would fall short of the overall nutritional demands of the fortress population.

▲ The moat surrounding the castle of Carcassonne, in south-western France. Note the wooden hoarding on the battlements. (Ad Meskens/CC-BY-SA-3.0)

▼ A panoramic photograph of the Nimrod Fortress on Mount Hermon, showing how the fortress acted as a sentinel over the valley below. (King/CC-BY-SA-3.0)

▼ This aerial view of Caerphilly Castle in South Wales illustrates the architect's intelligent use of waterworks to bolster the stone defences. (Cadw)

DEFENSIVE DESIGN

While natural obstacles could contribute to the fortress's security, the primary means of keeping out the enemy were the defences constructed as part of the fabric of the building complex itself. Here we enter into the complex realm of defensive design, which reached a state of high art in the late medieval and early Renaissance periods.

MOATS

The first layer of defence was likely to be one or more of a series of ditches or moats. Moats served the straightforward purpose of disrupting the movement of attackers both above ground and, if the moat was dug deep, underground, by interfering with undermining operations. The popular impression of a moat, particularly in Europe, is that of a minor artificial river surrounding a fortification. In fact, many moats were simply dry ditches ('dry ditch' is hence another term for such features), their defensive properties enhanced by embedding sharpened stakes and various other nasties in the bottom and sides.

When filled with water, the moat provided an added element of inertia; in the most sophisticated defensive arrangements, sluice gates were installed that allowed the castle commander to flood or empty the ditch, or at least

▶ *Bamburgh Castle on the east coast of Northumberland. Many fortresses are coastal in nature, using the sea as both protection and a route of resupply. (Henk Meijer/Alamy)*

▼ *Beaumaris Castle in North Wales is a fine specimen of concentric defences. Note the elevation of the inner walls over the outer curtain wall. (Cadw)*

▶ *A diagram from a French 19th-century architectural manual, showing the patterns of crenellation, the raised merlons featuring embrasures for archers. (PD)*

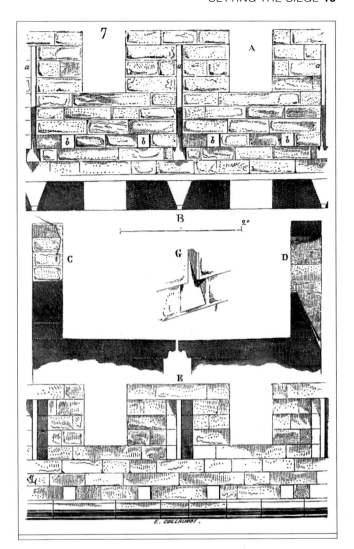

raise or lower the levels. A good example of this facility would be Beaumaris Castle in Angelsey, Wales, which had a moat fed from a nearby freshwater stream and sluice gates controlling the volume of water that could pass through into the ditch. At the extreme end of water defences we can place the epic Chittorgarh, a 7th-century hilltop fort near the Indian city of Udaipur. In total, the fortification was protected by no fewer than 84 individual bodies of surrounding water – 40 per cent of the entire complex's physical area.

OUTER WALLS

Attackers who managed to cross the ditches or moats (if they had to do so), then had to negotiate the most visible of a fortification's features; its external walls. For largely transparent reasons of defence, protection and deterrence, what we generally refer to as curtain walls (walls without structural purpose, but purely providing an outer defence) were built with formidable properties, e.g. long, strong and high.

A dependable curtain wall had to be thick and physically strong (to resist missiles, rams and other smashing devices), high (to prevent easy access, especially from escalade), defendable (the garrison had to be able to fight from its top and through its apertures) and with limited, defendable access points. Well back into early history, we find examples of imposing protective walls. Evacuations of the ancient city of Sardis, for example, have unearthed mud-brick walls some 20m (65ft 7in) thick and with extant sections standing 15m (49ft 3in) high. In China, Nanking's medieval city walls extended for more than 20km (12.4 miles) with a base thickness of up to 14.5m (47ft 7in) – although more in the region of 4.5m (14ft 9in) at the top – and a height of up to 21m (68ft 11in). (Fortification walls were typically thicker at the base to resist undermining and structural attacks; the flared portion, what is known as a *talus* or *batter*, also served to make rocks or other hand-dropped projectiles bounce outwards into the enemy, rather than simply slam straight into the mud.) The typical medieval European castle would have walls 10–20m (32ft 10in–65ft 7in) high and 4.5–6m (14ft 9in–19ft 8in) thick.

Defensive features

Walls, of course, provided only passive defence. Active defence came from the garrison, hence the walls had to be configured in such a way to provide them with cover and concealment from the blizzard of missiles that would inevitably come their way, plus spaces through which they could launch their own attacks or active defence. The very top of the fortress wall was typically formed into the

▶ *Wooden hoarding, set upon stone corbels, provided a means for defenders to attack the enemy directly at the base of the walls. (Jebulon/CC0)*

▲ *Machiolation began appearing in defensive architecture in the 13th century, and was particularly common in southern Europe and the Middle East. (Pearson Scott Foresman / PD).*

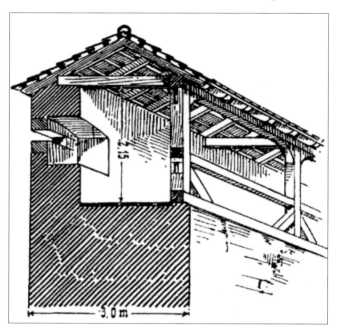

▲ *A cutaway of a 15th-century hoarding. Properly constructed, hoarding would form a semi-permanent element of the fortress structure. (PD)*

familiar crenellated battlements. The raised sections of wall (merlons) provided cover while interspersed crenels (hence 'crenellation') were spaces through which the defenders could fire missiles or drop objects. The crenels were often enclosed with hinged wooden shutters to provide additional protection for the defenders, and the entire battlement might be covered in a wooden hoarding to provide a covered walkway. Sometimes this hoarding would actually project out from the top of the wall, with hinged floor panels through which the defenders could directly engage the attackers below. In more sophisticated buildings, the projecting hoarding design might actually be built as part of the stonework itself, with the gaps between supporting corbels creating 'machiolation', particularly common in French castles but found globally in various locations and fortifications.

TOWERS AND PROJECTIONS

The outer walls of fortifications were rarely a uniform flat surface against which the defenders beat themselves. At regular intervals, curtain walls were punctuated by towers, barbican, bastions and other projections, particularly at the corners of walls and along very flat long sections. The designs of these features, though subject to considerable variation depending on location and period, generally had the same purposes: while they did provide some civilian rooms and functions internally, their main defensive role was to provide elevated and/or outward extended fighting platforms that enabled the defenders to enfilade long sections of the curtain wall, meaning that essentially there was nowhere for the defenders to hide. Castle towers could also form blocking points should attackers manage to ascend onto the battlements; by removing select

support beams inside the towers, the defenders could collapse the wooden floors, meaning that the attackers could not pass through the towers to adjacent walls.

THE GATEHOUSE

One of the most critical defensive areas of a curtain wall was, of course, the main entrance, typically a sturdy gate. As this was theoretically the point of easiest access to the interior of the castle, it usually bristled with defensive features. Access through the main gate was often restricted by the

▼ *Towers provided 360-degree defensive visibility. They also often incorporated practical features, such as water-collection guttering. (Pearson Scott Foresman/PD)*

use of a drawbridge that, when lowered, provided the only main crossing point over a moat or ditch. When the castle was under threat, the drawbridge could be raised via either winch and chain, a counterweight or a pivoting mechanism, closing off access to through the gatehouse. The gatehouse itself presented a lethal set of challenges for those who attempted to pass through its stony passage. A timber framed portcullis, reinforced with iron, plus a solid wooden door locked in place by a crossbeam, were resilient barriers and required destruction by either ramming or fire. The keeps on either side of the gatehouse might be replete with arrow slits so defenders could fire into the crowding masses of the attackers at point-blank range, while machiolation or 'murder holes' set above the entranceway were used to drop boulders, boiling oil and water, scalding sand, molten tar, quicklime and other grim substances down upon the attackers. Sometimes the gatehouse would be flanked by mighty barbican towers, well-defended structures that made the gatehouse area even more hostile for the attackers. The gatehouse would not be the only entrance or exit for the fortification. We are mainly using the terminology relating to Western castles here, but the principles would be applicable to all manner of fortifications across time and location.

▲ *A view upwards at the 'murder holes' at Bodiam Castle, East Sussex, England. Murder holes could also be used to pour water onto fires below. (Canadacow/CC-BY-3.0).*

GATEHOUSE AND DRAWBRIDGE

In this graphic representation of a gatehouse, we see a model of the interrelationship between the drawbridge and the portcullis behind it. During a siege, the drawbridge would be raised and the portcullis lowered, together forming combined barriers to access through the gatehouse. Here the systems used for operating the two features are pulley-assisted winding mechanisms.

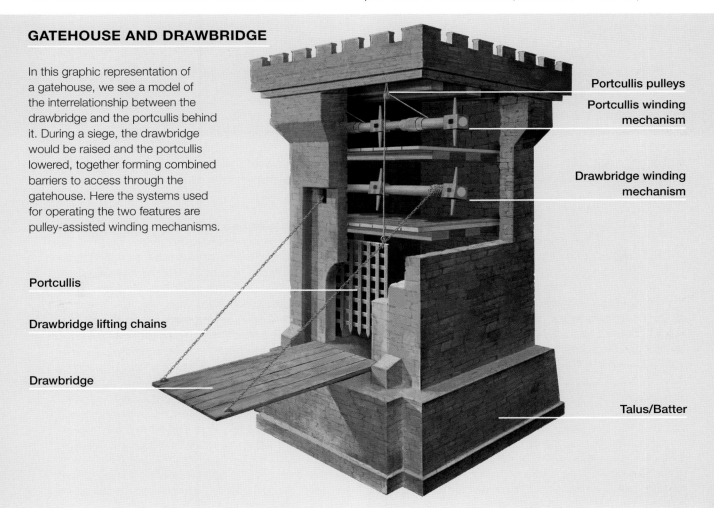

Portcullis pulleys

Portcullis winding mechanism

Drawbridge winding mechanism

Portcullis

Drawbridge lifting chains

Drawbridge

Talus/Batter

▲ *The gatehouse of Carisbrooke castle on the Isle of Wight. The gateway section of the castle was erected in 1464 by Lord Scales. (Nilfanion/CC BY-SA 3.0)*

Postern gates and ports

Minor postern gates and sally ports provided further points of entrance and egress, although recognising that these features were vulnerabilities as much as utilities, they were frequently concealed in the fabric of the building, or blended into natural features. Should a treacherous local betray the presence of a sally port to the besieging army, then invasive disaster might rapidly overtake the fortification. In some fortress, natural entrances might be created by an inflowing waterway or a natural cavern beneath the castle; any and all such points needed zealous concealment. But they were integral parts of the castle's defence. In particular, the sally ports enabled garrison troops to venture out rapidly beyond the castle walls to attack siege engines or enemy sappers, retreating quickly back within the castle's protective walls once the assault was delivered.

◄ *A sally port set in the curtain wall of the French fortress. Note how the port is tucked into the angle of a tower, to obscure its view to others. (Thesupermat/GFDL).*

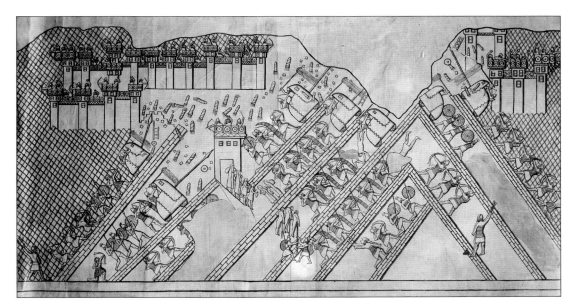

► *This striking artwork shows the siege of Lachish (701 BC) in Israel, with the artwork vividly depicting the multi-layered defences of the city's population and the Assyrian attackers utilising battering rams to make a breach. (Wellcome Images/CC-BY-4.0)*

INNER WALLS

Another defensive castle design was simply to multiply the number of walls the attackers had to negotiate. To optimise the defensive arrangements in multi-wall designs, the inner walls were typically higher than the outer walls – this allowed the defenders of the inner walls to fire down upon attackers as they surmounted the outer walls. Ancient examples of fortresses with multiple curtain walls include the city of Lachish in modern-day Israeli, fortified from the 9th century BC with substantial rings of walls. Surviving artistic representations of these walls, depicting the fall of the fortress to the Assyrians in 701 BC, show inner and outer walls, all heavily accented with defensive towers from which archers rain down arrows on

the assaulting Assyrians, the inner walls standing proud of the outer walls to provide clear fields of fire to all archers. During the medieval period in Europe, the 'concentric castle' became a popular style of defensive layout, with the space between the outer and inner curtain walls creating the 'inner bailey' area (as opposed to the 'outer bailey' beyond the outermost wall), effectively a kill zone for attackers unfortunate enough to be trapped there. Good examples of concentric castles include the aforementioned Krak des Chevaliers and Beaumaris Castle.

▼ *A plan of Harlech castle in Wales. Note how the towers and the gatehouse barbican provide perfect enfilade along the inner walls. (Cadw)*

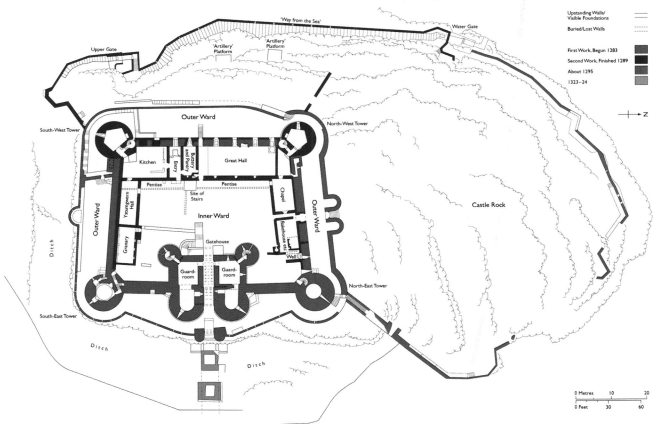

INNER DEFENCES

Above all, the priority of a fortress garrison was to prevent an enemy ascending, tunnelling under or breaching the curtain walls. If he did so, and entered into the fortress interior, then the options were generally to fight to the death or to capitulate immediately and throw yourself on the attackers' mercy – the latter was never a sure thing after the intense emotional release of a fortress assault.

FIRE AND WATER

Walking around the remnants of fortresses and castles today, visitors can be misled by the now-empty courtyards or baileys. In their heyday, the inner spaces of a fortress were usually places of humming human activity, filled with wooden domestic buildings, stables, storage areas, barracks, markets and many other places of life and work. The presence of these structures was the main reason why fire was such a threat to fortresses; incendiary arrows or pots of flammable materials could, if dropped accurately amongst the wooden frameworks, spread serious and uncontrollable fire.

An added complication for the inhabitants of the fortress was that the siege conditions often left water in short supply, with no surplus on standby for putting out major fires. During the siege of Exeter Castle in 1136, besieged for three months by King Stephen, wine had to be used to quench fires from incendiary arrows, with water too valuable to use for such purposes.

Indeed, the issue of water supply could be the deciding factor in the outcome of a siege, for both sides, especially in arid territories such as the Middle East or during hot, dry summers. Some fortresses would have internal wells, and most would also have rainwater harvesting systems built atop towers, the sloping roofs channelling the rainwater down via gutters and drainpipes into a stone cistern. Yet if the rains did not come, or if the besiegers managed to divert or poison an important water source for the inhabitants, defeat could come within days.

THE KEEP

The chaos and horror that could be unleashed once invaders entered the inner areas of a fortress can only be imagined. In major fortified cities, something akin to a large-scale urban street battle could ensue, with the surviving members of the garrison and spirited civilians resisting the enemy in alleyways, domestic rooms and small courtyards. Yet for the fortunate few, there might be further places of retreat. Many fortresses had major defensive structures within their inner walls, consisting of walled citadels, towers, minor forts or huge block-like keeps. The 13th-century Château de Coucy in

◄ *Caernarvon Castle in North Wales featured curtain walls that were a stupendous 6m (20ft) thick in places, with no fewer than 12 towers to provide the defenders with vantage points. (Cadw)*

▶ *This plan of Beaumaris Castle, with an intricate concentric layout, illustrates the sophistication that castle layouts achieved during the medieval period. (Cadw)*

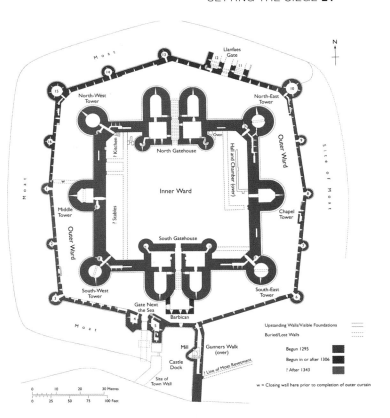

Picardy, France, for example, had an inner *donjon* (keep) that was 34m (111ft 7in) wide by 55m (180ft 5in) tall. Many British castles have similarly substantial keeps. Into such redoubts the great and the good, plus defending soldiery, might retreat for a last stand, or at least to buy some time for negotiated surrender. They might also, alternatively, attempt to make their escape through any hidden underground passages or tunnels that remained unknown to their attackers. During recent archaeological excavations of the castle in Sławków (Silesia), historians have found two hidden escape tunnels deep beneath the main structure, long enough to allow escape well beyond the walls in the event of a siege.

As this short overview indicates, fortresses are by their very nature designed and adapted to keep even the most persistent of enemies out. Furthermore, the fact that the garrison would also rely on force of arms to repel attackers, and not just on walls and physical obstacles, shows that fortresses or castles were centres of *active* defence, not a passive and compliant withdrawal. Overcoming both the physical and the human resistance was the combined challenge for the besieging army and its commanders.

▼ *The Old West sally port in Edinburgh Castle. Note the rough, steep ground in the foreground, a natural barrier to the free movement of attackers. (Kim Traynor/CC BY-SA 3.0)*

▼ *The Château de Coucy in France was built in the 1220s by Enguerrand III, Lord of Coucy. Its prodigious keep is seen in the foreground. (PD)*

LAYING THE SIEGE

Sieges were rarely preferred choices for military commanders. Even more so than a pitched battle or a planned ambush, besieging a fortress or walled city was a commitment to something that was impossible to predict. How much time would be needed, how much money would be spent, was very difficult to estimate – a huge problem when professional armies rarely existed.

With some exceptions, up until the late Renaissance most states and empires relied on part-time citizen armies, drawn into service as and when they were needed. As societies were largely agrarian in nature during our period, pulling away large amounts of manpower from the land to engage in a prolonged siege could have a deleterious effect on a state's crop production. It was for this reason that military campaigns in ancient and medieval times were largely seasonal affairs, launched and hopefully completed in the summer to avoid planting and harvesting activities. Sieges, however, had a nasty habit of running on well beyond seasonal limits.

FINANCE

Furthermore, the king, queen or commander intending to engage in a siege had to account for some serious budget considerations. Military personnel alone brought with them dramatically escalating expenses. For example, in Archaic

▼ *A modern depiction of a Roman siege, showing multiple siege engines in action. (Lebrecht Library/Alamy).*

and Classical Athens, the cost of a day's service of an Athenian hoplite was two drachmas. Historian Konstantin Nossov has noted that 'With 3,000 hoplites brought into the siege of Potidaea, each day of the siege cost Athens 6,000 drachmas (one talent) for the hoplites alone. The siege, which lasted over two years, was worth 2,000 talents. Compare this figure to Athens' annual income, which was about 6,000 talents.[1] The situation was no better in the medieval period. The feudal military service of a vassal or knight to his lord had variable annual limits, typically 40 days but instances as low as 20 days or as high as 90 days are recorded. Beyond these limits, therefore, the ruler had to pay for each additional day's service from out of his personal or state coffers, which could deplete at an horrendous rate. (Even today in the UK, British citizens still pay certain taxes that were only introduced in the first place to cover the costs of dynastic or religious wars.)

BACK-UP

But a siege was not just a matter of marching an army to the enemy's city walls. Sieges by their very nature were

▲ *A Spanish artwork showing a 13th-century siege in action. Note what appears to be a traction trebuchet in the bottom corner. (Granger Historical Picture Archive/Alamy)*

materially and physically demanding events. One of the best documented is the siege of Bedford Castle in 1224, launched by King Henry III (r. 1216–72) in an attempt to wrest the fortification from the hands of the rebellious Anglo-Norman ruler Falkes de Breauté. Bedford Castle – a formidable piece of medieval real estate – promised no easy victory, so Henry put together a massive force. It was not just soldiers who were required. Henry's army included carpenters (to construct and maintain siege engines), rope-makers, stone masons (to make stone siege engine ammunition, which also had to be quarried specially for the siege), cooks, blacksmiths and miners (for undermining operations). He purchased huge quantities of goods, including hides, rope, tallow, leather, charcoal and vast numbers of crossbow bolts, possibly 43,300 in total, plus all the accoutrements necessary for setting up a camp – tents, candles, fodder for horses and the tools to assemble everything required. In total, some 1,600 to 2,700 men were required every single day for a period of eight weeks, which, when added to the material investment came to £1,311. Converting such money to current values is problematic, but there wouldn't have been too much change from £800,000 in today's money.

TIME

So, time and money were critical considerations in establishing and maintaining a siege. Time was especially pressing. The commander of the besieging army had to bring the siege to as swift a conclusion as possible – if it dragged on for many months, beyond the classic campaigning season, then, depending on the theatre, the army would be subjected to the physical depredations of the autumn and winter months, and the prolonged drain on logistics that could reduce men to thin rations and equally thin bodies. There was also the issue of maintaining the soldiers' mental state, to keep them fit for assault. Prolonged sieges tended to breed apathy, sickness, boredom and dissolution, never core qualities of an effective siege army.

▲ *A medieval German depiction of a siege camp, the besieging army living in spartan but orderly tent barracks outside the city walls. (PD)*

▶ *The siege of Rouen by Henry V, 1418–19. In total, Henry set up four fortified camps around the city. (Lebrecht Music and Arts Photo Library/Alamy)*

SIEGE TACTICS

Once the siege had been laid, the army encamped, watches set and local terrain surveyed, a strategy had to be decided upon. Boiled down to basics, the commander of a besieging army essentially had three options for bringing the siege to a conclusion (i.e. taking the enemy fortress) – diplomacy, passive attrition or assault.

DIPLOMACY

This was by far the preferable route, involving little sacrifice of men and resources with maximum return. The form the diplomacy could take varied. Sometimes just the sheer visual threat of an enveloping siege army could persuade a fortress commander to seek terms quickly, remembering the point that if the fortress garrison chose to resist, they typically gave up already uncertain future rights to clemency, should the opponents breach the walls and enter inside.

Surrender

The expeditionary Roman emperor Julius Caesar (r. 49–15 BC) was particularly lucid in offering rebellious towns and fortresses clear terms. During his sweep through Gaul, he gave the populations in his way a sharp option – surrender before any military action was taken, and the population would be spared. Resist, and face bloody retribution. Towns such as Vellaunodunum and Noviodunum took the opt-out clause, and hence were spared the Roman sword.

In medieval Europe, once the chivalric code had taken root, the besieging commander would similarly call upon the resisting fortress to surrender as an early option – if they did so, then the garrison and civilians would be allowed to march out from the fortress unmolested and with honour. A problem arose if the fortress commander at the time of the siege felt he did not have the authority to make a decision about future strategy, usually if he had to consult upwards to a higher and absent authority.

Some commanders could, and did, ask for a temporary truce while they found their leader and clarified terms, but medieval communications being what they were, the commander might well have to act on his own judgement. For example, in 1118 King Henry I's bastion at La Motte-Gautier-de-Clinchamp in Maine, France, was placed under siege by Fulk, Count of Anjou, who subjected the castle to both bombardment from siege engines and regular assaults. The 140-man garrison of knights remained initially resistant and unharmed, but saw the writing on the wall

▼ *The siege of Plataea, Greece, in 429–427 BC. This artwork gives an impression of the elaborate encircling walls built by the Spartans. (Chronicle/Alamy)*

▶ *The brutal aftermath of a siege, with civilians and ruler (indicated by the crown on one of the decapitated heads) being put to the sword without mercy. (Getty)*

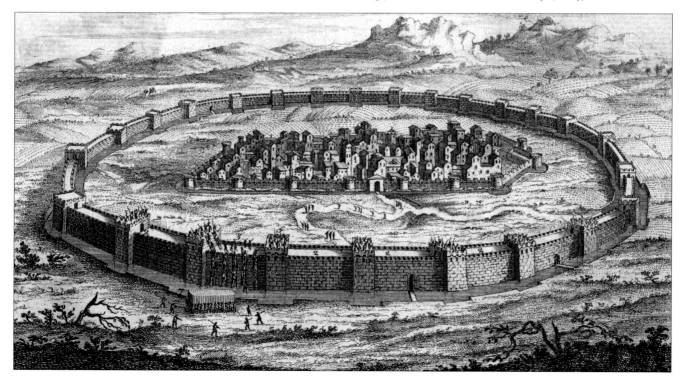

◄ A photograph of Pembroke Castle in South Wales, taken in 1905. The extensive castle was developed from a Norman motte-and-bailey design, with periodic rebuilding over a period of three centuries. (LOC)

and attempted to contact Henry for guidance on the matter. This contact failing, the garrison commander eventually surrendered the castle, an act which incensed Henry. The commander defended himself by saying that there was no instruction from the king nor any evidence that a relief force was on its way.

▼ Siege of Dapur by the army of Rameses II in 1269 BC. Note how the archer, covered by infantry shields, provides supporting fire for the escalade. (PD)

PASSIVE ATTRITION

If a fortress did not make an immediate surrender, then the siege was on. If the fortress were not taken immediately in an immediate assault, then the baseline tactic was to isolate it from the outside world, and let starvation, thirst and fear work to break the defence without an arrow being fired or a stone being hurled. This approach was perfectly logical, but did not necessarily stack the odds of victory in the favour of the besiegers. Even with a swift march, the advance of a besieging army could be a ponderous affair, giving the fortress population time to prepare for their investment. Food would be stockpiled and meats would be dried or salted to give them longevity in storage. Space allowing, livestock and fodder would be taken into the fortress from the surrounding fields. Conversely, the surrounding area might be stripped of anything that could profit the attackers. Defensive weaponry was constructed and

▼ Canon made an appearance at the siege of Rouen by the British in 1419. The wheeled gun carriage at the back is anachronistic. (PD)

stockpiled. A particularly ruthless ruler might expel anyone from the fortress who was deemed an unnecessary drain on resources (i.e. non-combatants), doing this both before and during a siege. This practice led to some wearying horrors, with civilians of all ages simply dying of exposure and starvation between the fortress walls and the inner siege lines. Examples are found in the siege of Château Gaillard in 1202–4 and the siege of Rouen in 1418–19 (see Chapter 6).

Deprivation

A besieged fortress might well resist for many months, even years, if it was intelligently stocked, had a manageable number of mouths to feed, was favoured by the weather (particularly in terms of receiving rainfall to collect water) and had sufficient firepower and manpower to hold out against assault. Yet, typically, sieges did impose the most horrible deprivations on a population. At the aforementioned siege of Rouen, the desolate citizens were forced to eat dogs, cats, rats and mice; even supplies of those soon ran out. During the Roman siege of Athens in 87–86 BC, boiled leather featured on the daily menu. Even reports of cannibalism haunt the very darkest corners of some siege narratives. It should be noted, however, that the attackers might also be prey to starvation, particularly if the siege was conducted in a territory with a harsh climate and little in the way of natural

▼ *The defensive walls of Dubrovnik, Croatia, still appear imposing. The Minceta Tower in the centre became a powerful gun platform. (Romanceor/CC BY-SA 3.0)*

resources. The ideal outcome for the besiegers was to reduce the population to such depravity that they were forced to surrender. The objective for the fortress commander, by contrast, was to hold out long enough that his enemies were compelled to call off their siege, or to give time for a relieving army to reach and rescue them.

ISOLATION AND CONTAINMENT

Naturally, if a siege was to be truly effective, then the invested fortress had to be cut off from the outside world. To do this, siege lines would be built, from which the attackers could ensure that no one could pass in or out of the fortress, and from which the besieging forces could both launch attacks against the fortress and repel attacks from outside it. At its most basic, for a minor siege, the siege lines might consist of little more than a ditch cut around the fortress and bolstered by a wooden palisade. Yet in many cases, siege lines could be major constructions in their own right.

Early pioneers of the technique of structural containment were the Athenians, who during the 5th century BC perfected the art of *periteichismos* (encirclement). Stone masons, labourers and carpenters who accompanied the Greek army would build full encircling walls, typically of a dry stone construction with a timber wall-walk and battlements, punctuated by great wooden towers. In many ways, these walls mirrored the curtain walls facing the attackers, and they required much time, effort and resources to raise. The defenders, seeing the trap growing around them, might opt for early offensive action in an attempt to disrupt the building

Inaccessible locations were some of the best defensive features of ancient and medieval fortresses. Here we see Château Gaillard ('strong castle'), built by Richard I of England, set high on a rocky plateau above the commune of Les Andelys in Normandy, France. (Shutterstock)

work. At the Athenian siege of Syracuse (415–13 BC), for example, the Athenians began to construct a major double-wall *periteichismos* around the city. Thucydides, in his *History of the Peloponnesian War*, noted how this effort scalded the Syracusans into action: 'The Syracusans, appalled at the rapidity with which the work advanced, determined to go out against them and give battle and interrupt it; and the two armies were already in battle array, when the Syracusan generals observed that their troops found such difficulty in getting into line, and were in such disorder, that they led them back into the town, except part of the cavalry. These remained and hindered the Athenians from carrying stones or dispersing to any great distance, until a tribe of the Athenian heavy infantry, with all the cavalry, charged and routed the Syracusan horse with some loss.'[2]

▼ *This aerial view shows the remnants of one of several Roman legionary siege camps outside the circumvallation wall around the Masada fortress. (David Wei/Alamy)*

▲ *The siege of Numantia (134–33 BC) during Rome's Celtiberian Wars was famous for Scipio's impressive circumvallation of the city. (Lanmas/Alamy)*

Circumvallation and contravallation

The practice of building major siege lines around a fortress continued throughout ancient history and Roman imperial ascendancy, and across the medieval period. When time and resources allowed, the Romans (and some later medieval commanders) favoured constructing two parallel siege lines. The inner line, known as the line of *circumvallation*, was closest to the besieged fortress and featured a moat, stone wall with walkway and battlements, and defensive towers. Archaeological investigation has given us an impression of the might of these walls.

At the siege of Numantia by Scipio Aemilianus in 133 BC, the depth of the wall – at least in the sections explored – measured around 4.7m (15ft 5in), with a wall height of more than 3m (9ft 11in) and a walkway 2.4m (7ft 10in) wide. Every 30m (98ft 5in) or so would be a tower. The total length of these defences could have been in the region of 9km (5.6 miles) long, although some of these defences might have been made purely of wood.[3]

On the open ground in front of the circumvallation would be various embedded obstacles, to make the approaches to the Roman lines even more hazardous for any enemy attempting a sortie. Fire-hardened stakes and sharpened sections of branches stuck into the ground and angled towards the enemy broke up lines of approach, and 'lily' traps – concealed pits about 90cm (2ft 11in) deep with sharpened stakes, lightly concealed by foliage – wrecked the legs of men and horses alike when trod upon.

The outer wall in the siege works was known as the line of *contravallation*. (Note that the second line of siege works was not always constructed by the Romans nor by medieval siege commanders. Contravallation usually only emerged

SIEGE LINES

Life around and between the siege walls could take on a vitality akin to that of a small town, as literally thousands of soldiers turned the siege lines into their place of work, habitation, socialising and commerce, particularly over a long period. In Edward III's siege of Calais in 1346–47, for example, the British soldiers erected an area of wood and brushwood thatch housing, arranged in a logical and ordered street plan. To sustain this army, the martial camp then gained a fully fledged marketplace, which came to sell everything the soldiers needed for sustenance and military provisions. Indeed, such was the scale the town achieved – eventually some 30,000 people (soldiers and civilians) were crammed into its streets – that it acquired the status and the name of a fully fledged town, Villeneuve la Hardie.

▲ *Sometimes entire cities were protected by curtain walls. Here we see the walls of Avila, Spain, with a perimeter of 2,516m (2,752yds). (diego_cue/CC BY-SA 3.0)*

on the basis of necessity and time.) This wall could have an equal structural weighting as the inner wall, and with the same external defensive features in the ground, although naturally facing outwards away from the fortification, rather than inwards.

In medieval warfare the siege commander might, in preference to erecting siege lines, build a form of temporary castle or great tower near the besieged fortress. This created a strange mirror-like warfare, with two castles confronting one another and each vying for dominance. During the siege of Huntingdon in 1174 by Richard de Luci, the siege forces built a motte-and-bailey castle about 350m (383yds) away from the fortress, dismantling it once the siege was successfully won. If the siege force couldn't be bothered to go to the effort of making their own castle, then sometimes a nearby church tower was utilised as a fighting platform for siege engines and troops (churches were typically positioned near to fortress walls, to reinforce the connection between feudal military muscle and the divinely ordained social 'chain of being').

BETRAYAL AND BRIBERY

Sieges were tense and suspicious affairs for the besieged, as there was always the chance that individuals or groups within the walls might save themselves by betraying those around them, and besieging forces often dangled the carrots of bribery. We must also remember that there might be little sense of loyalty between town and garrison in many places, especially if the local lord was known for a particularly oppressive rule. Typical forms of betrayal might include revealing secret access points to attackers, betraying details about weakly guarded parts of the fortress, or simply agreeing to unlock a gate at a particular moment.

An unsettling example comes from the siege of Gabii in the 6th-century BC. The final Roman king, Lucius Tarquinius Superbus (r. 535–509 BC), head of the besieging army, was frustrated at the duration of his campaign against rebellious Latin states, and opted for guile to prize the city of Gabii open. While simultaneously pretending to have lost interest in the siege, he beat his own son, Sextus, who then went over to the Gabii bearing his wounds on the pretence that he wanted to swap sides. The Gabii took Sextus into their midst, and he then promptly betrayed their confidence, using his influence to

◄ *The ruins of a moat in the Ancient Greek Eurialo castle, in Syracuse, Sicily. The pillars at the back were for a drawbridge. (GNUFDL)*

▲ Built on the orders of King Henry VIII in the 16th century, Deal Castle was a coastal artillery fortress, offering a total of 66 firing positions. (Lieven Smits/CC BY-SA 3.0)

have the leaders of the city executed then effectively forcing the population to capitulate and open their doors to Tarquinius.

If an entrance could not be made by pulling the levers of guile or duplicity, then it was a matter of direct force.

▼ A reconstruction of one of the Roman guard towers built along the wall of circumvallation at the siege of Alesia in 52 BC. (Christophe Finot/CC BY-SA 2.5)

THE EFFECTS OF DISEASE

Disease could be one of the deciding factors in a siege action, afflicting the forces on both sides of the siege lines. The very nature of siege warfare often quickly led to unhealthy conditions both inside and outside the fortress. Water and food supplies could quickly become contaminated, especially once sanitation became compromised by ineffective disposal of human waste and from the constant presence of corpses and wounds. (The besieged inside a fortress would have a particular challenge in disposing of their dead.) The three principal health curses of siege warfare were dysentery, cholera and typhus, and once these established themselves they could account for more casualties than the fighting itself. Both could take hold with grim rapidity. During the siege of Harfleur, France, which was invested for just five weeks in 1415 by the English forces of King Henry V, an estimated 1,330 English soldiers had to be invalided home with the 'bloody flux' (dysentery), which the defenders had encouraged by opening the sluice gates around the town, flooding the surrounding fields and fostering the easy spread of water-borne diseases. Besieging armies could also make active measures to encourage disease, not least by hurling rotting and infected corpses over the city walls in an early act of biological warfare. For example, the city of Caffa, in present-day Ukraine, was besieged by Mongol forces in 1345–46, just as the Black Death plague was ripping Europe and Asia apart. Although the disease eventually broke the Mongol siege through escalating fatalities, the Mongols decided to share the misery and the death by hurling their corpses into the city. The effects were horrific: 'What seemed like mountains of dead were thrown into the city, and the Christians could not hide or flee or escape from them, although they dumped as many bodies as they could into the sea. As soon as the rotting corpses tainted the air and poisoned the water supply, and the stench was so overwhelming that hardly one in several thousand was in a position to flee the remains of the Tartar army. Moreover one infected man could carry the poison to others, and infect people and places with the disease by look alone. No one knew, or could discover, a means of defence.'[5] One top of plague and diseases of sanitation, sieges in tropical parts of the world also had to cope with the spectrum of threats borne by insects and parasites. European warriors on the Crusades, for example, suffered from blights such as malaria, gastrointestinal parasites and trachoma (a severe eye infection, potentially leading to blindness). In addition, siege forces might even suffer from scurvy, as supplies of fresh fruit and vegetables ran out.

JULIUS CAESAR'S SIEGE OF ALESIA

The siege of Alesia was a landmark action in Julius Caesar's vicious and wearing campaign to secure Gaul in 58–50 BC. The siege began in July 52 BC, when a huge force of Gallic warriors – 80,000 infantry and 50,000 cavalry – under the command of the great leader Vercingetorix, took refuge in the imposing fortress town of Alesia, near modern Alise-Ste.Reine, France. The fortress itself presented a daunting challenge for even as talented a commander as Caesar – it towered above the battlefield on Mount Auxois, with steep cliffs, rivers (running around the base of the mountain) and defensive ditches making for a hazardous approach. Nevertheless, Caesar and his men tackled the challenge with ingenuity and industry. The following description by Caesar himself, written characteristically in the third person in his *Gallic Wars*, describes the specific measures of emplacing the siege:

> Caesar [...] adopted the following system of fortification; he dug a trench twenty feet [6m] deep, with perpendicular sides, in such a manner that the base of this trench should extend so far as the edges were apart at the top. He raised all his other works at a distance of four hundred feet [122m] from that ditch; [he did] that with this intention, lest (since he necessarily embraced so extensive an area, and the whole works could not be easily surrounded by a line of soldiers) a large number of the enemy should suddenly, or by night, sally against the fortifications; or lest they should by day cast weapons against our men while occupied with the works. Having left this interval, he drew two

trenches fifteen feet [4.5m] broad, and of the same depth; the innermost of them, being in low and level ground, he filled with water conveyed from the river. Behind these he raised a rampart and wall twelve feet [3.7m] high; to this he added a parapet and battlements, with large stakes cut like stags' horns, projecting from the junction of the parapet and battlements, to prevent the enemy from scaling it, and surrounded the entire work with turrets, which were eighty feet [24m] distant from one another.

[...] Caesar thought that further additions should be made to these works, in order that the fortifications might be defensible by a small number of soldiers. Having, therefore, cut down the trunks of trees or very thick branches, and having stripped their tops of the bark, and sharpened them into a point, he drew a continued trench everywhere five feet [1.5m] deep. These stakes being sunk into this trench, and fastened firmly at the bottom, to prevent the possibility of their being torn up, had their branches only projecting from the ground. There were five rows in connection with, and intersecting each other; and whoever entered within them were likely to impale themselves on very sharp stakes. The soldiers called these *cippi*. Before these, which were arranged in oblique rows in the form of a quincunx, pits three feet [90cm] deep were dug, which gradually diminished in depth to the bottom. In these pits tapering stakes, of the thickness of a man's thigh, sharpened at the top and hardened in the fire, were sunk in such a manner as to project from the ground not more than four inches; at the same time for the purpose of giving them strength and stability, they were each filled with trampled clay to the height of one foot [30cm] from the bottom: the rest of the pit was covered over with osiers

▼ *A map of the siege of Alesia, which shows how the Romans intelligently incorporated the path of rivers into their siege lines. (US Gov/PD)*

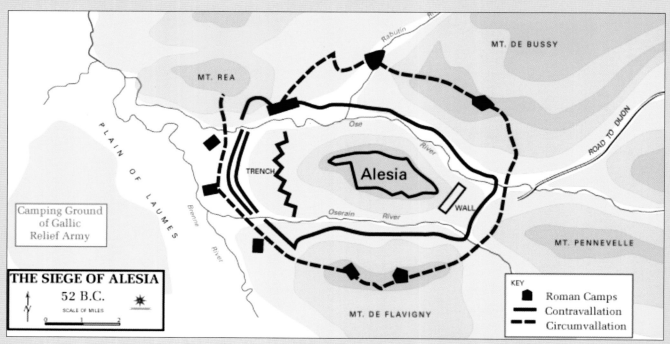

and twigs, to conceal the deceit. Eight rows of this kind were dug, and were three feet distant from each other. They called this a 'lily' from its resemblance to that flower. Stakes a foot long, with iron hooks attached to them, were entirely sunk in the ground before these, and were planted in every place at small intervals; these they called spurs.[4]

Note the sheer sophistication of the Roman siege works, which included moats and ditches, a defendable wall system and ground-emplaced anti-personnel features. Through 22.5km (14 miles) of such works, Caesar both trapped the

▲ *Roman troops set to work with industry while constructing the siege lines around Alesia. The circumvallation proved essential to fight off Gallic counterattacks. (Getty)*

garrison of Alesia and protected his own troops from Gallic relief attacks. These measures proved circumspect, as in October the Romans came under repeated assaults from a vast Gallic relief force. Caesar's legions fought off three immense attacks, eventually breaking the Gallic offensive and compelling the relief force to flee. With his people now starving, Vercingetorix saw the inevitable, and surrendered.

▶ *The multi-layer Roman ground defences at Alesia, here consisting of a double-trench, two rows of sharpened branches and a ditch at the foot of the rampart. (Carole Raddato/ CC BY-SA 2.0)*

PHYSICAL ATTACK

If diplomacy and prolonged attrition didn't bring the fortress to its knees, then force was the only remaining option. Indeed, force might well have been the besieging army's very first action, if they wanted to retain the element of surprise and enforce the initiative, they were convinced they were the superior force, or if they were just plain out of patience or mercy.

Having a reputation for swift attacks was no doubt an advantage in successful siege warfare. During the early decades of the Republic a Roman army was often inclined to throw troops at a fortress in a rapid escalade assault, often with success, although the tactic was probably influenced by the fact that at this stage in their military evolution they were less experienced in passive siege techniques than their enemies. Siege warfare force options are the focus of the subsequent chapters in this book, so only an overview will be provided here. There were basically three options for getting into a fortress – go through, go under, go over.

▼ *During the Ostrogothic siege of Rome in 540 BC, the Roman defenders resorted to throwing ornamental masonry at their attackers. (Bildagentur/Alamy)*

Go through would mean either:
1) using duplicity or traitors to gain access into the fortress;
2) breaching the main doors;
3) breaching the main walls with artillery or sappers.

BREACHING THE OUTER WALLS

To breach fortress walls or gates directly required a combination of siege engines and manpower. Battering rams could be used to fracture walls or splinter wood, with the repeated impacts of the ram head eventually producing an access point, as long as the ram operators and the engines themselves could survive the countermeasures of the defenders. There were also options such as boring engines, which ground through wood or stone with a drill-like bit, and various types of claw devices for ripping away at masonry or

the frame of a portcullis. Alternatively, or additionally, the siege force could resort to the use of bolt-firing and stone-lobbing siege artillery, to strike at the walls repeatedly from distances of up to several hundred metres, in the case of the largest specimens.

Such weapons offered the advantages of stand-off distance, reasonably dependable structural attrition, high-trajectory attacks directly against the defenders and buildings inside the castle and, with enough weight of fire, a crumbled curtain wall or broken tower. But siege engines of any variety were expensive and time-consuming to construct and demanded intensive volumes of manpower to operate; if they couldn't be borrowed or purchased from a sympathetic state or lord, they would generally be constructed in situ at the siege, a process that could take several weeks before missiles were actually launched. Of course, the role of artillery in siege warfare was revolutionised by the advent of gunpowder artillery in the 14th century, with the new weapon bringing far greater direct-fire effects on fortress walls and structures.

▼ *The Romans came to master the art of siege warfare. Here siege artillery assaults the battlements while a siege tower and escalade make the assault. (Alamy)*

▲ *A 16th-century depiction of a siege, showing the moment when the city is sacked by the attackers, the cannon in the foreground having done their work. (Ivy Close Images/Alamy)*

An alternative method of bringing down walls was sapping. Here, hardy labourers, armed with little more than hammers, chisels and props, would be deployed at the face of a fortress wall, usually under the cover of a mobile shelter or via a wood-covered trench (a 'sap') dug out from the siege lines. Once at the wall, they would proceed to hack out supporting masonry or dig holes into the earth beneath, holding up the wall above as they went with wooden struts. When the time was right, fire was set around the wooden struts, and once those burned through and collapsed, the wall would – if all was done properly – come down, creating a breach that would be directly assaulted.

Incidentally, fire was a particularly useful tool as a siege weapon for both sides (see Chapter 7). Incendiary missiles and compounds could be used to set fire to wooden structures within a fortress, or to weaken a wooden fortress door structurally, thereby leaving it vulnerable to the impacts of the battering ram. The means of fire-starting were many and sometimes ingenious, from simple fire arrows through to heated metal missiles, pots of incendiary mixtures and even rudimentary flamethrowers hurling 'Greek fire' under the pressure of air bellows. Given that wooden siege towers, siege engines and protective palisades were all used by besieging forces, the fear of fire went both ways.

▲ *Dover Castle exhibits the square towers often seen in the pre-artillery age; rounded or angular towers and bastions were more resistant to cannon shot.*

▼ *An artist's impression of the siege of Dover Castle in 1216–17. The castle's defences held out against the French over a 10-month siege. (Heritage Image Partnership Ltd/Alamy)*

MINING

If direct access through a wall or door proved challenging, there was always the 'under' option, which basically referred to the activity of 'undermining'. In this highly hazardous practice, a mine shaft was cut out from the siege lines and developed into a wood-supported tunnel directly beneath the fortress wall. As with the sapping techniques, the supports were then destroyed by fire (or later by gunpowder explosion), bringing a collapse of the wall above. Mining was an arduous business, and relied upon access to experienced personnel and also the nature of the terrain – extensive water defences or the fortification sitting on a solid rock plateau could rule out mining as an option. Also take into account that the fortress garrison could dig their own mines from the inside out, either as part of a counter-mining activity or as a form of underground sortie against the enemy forces.

SCALING THE WALLS

The final option for the siege forces was to go 'over', and that meant one or a combination of tactics. Chief amongst these was 'escalade', literally attempting to climb the walls with assault ladders thrown quickly over the battlements. The obvious peril to this approach was that, while climbing, the assaulting soldier was exposed to missiles dropped from above and also to the ladders being dislodged. Nevertheless, performed skilfully, quickly and with suppressive fire from supporting troops on the ground, escalade could be a very successful tactic.

There were some other options, however, that required a little more industry. First, siege towers – literally giant wheeled wooden towers containing men and siege engines – could be trundled up to the battlements, from which platforms could be dropped to bridge the gap between tower and fortress. Second, the besieging engineers and labours could create a sloping earthen embankment that ran from ground level up to a high level on the facing wall. This embankment would then be used for deploying siege engines higher up the wall defences, and for providing a shorter distance to the battlements for assaulting troops. The embankment tactic tended to be more characteristic of the ancient period than the medieval period.

This whirlwind tour of siege warfare tactics provides an immediate theoretical foundation for what follows. For, as we shall see, the outcome of a siege was dependent on a bewildering range of technical and human considerations that stretched the resourcefulness of both sides to the limit.

▼ *The aftermath of a siege could be brutal in the extreme. Here townsfolk are hanged and beheaded after the siege of Haarlem, 1573. (Lanmas/Alamy)*

HAERLEM

2

BRUTE FORCE: BATTERING RAMS AND BORERS

Fortress gates and walls were purposely designed to keep attackers out, through a combination of height, physical solidity and defendable positions. If a besieging army was to make a breach in such defences, they needed impact weapons with power and durability.

◄ *A besieging army brings up two A-frame battering rams to assault the fortress walls. By smashing lower parts of the masonry, it was hoped that the wall would eventually collapse under its own weight. (Getty)*

BATTERING RAMS

Even today, ancient and medieval fortresses convey an impression of impregnability, the depth and height of their walls making human strength look irrelevant in comparison. Yet muscle power combined with basic physics meant that with time and persistence, even the mightiest bastion could be toppled.

In this chapter, our focus will be on what at first glance is the most elementary of the siege engines – battering rams. Sitting next to the torsion firepower of a ballista or the towering frame of a trebuchet, battering rams can appear almost like last-ditch weapons, for the moment when the besieging army has nothing left to use except brute force. Certainly, battering rams can be some of the very simplest weapons in the siege arsenal, yet this was not always the case. In fact, some battering rams rivalled any other mechanisms on the battlefield in terms of complexity and tactical relevance.

TIME, FORCE AND DEFENCE

The battering ram is essentially a textbook demonstration of Newton's First Law of Motion, or the Law of Inertia, which states, 'An object at rest stays at rest and an object in motion stays in motion with the same speed and in the same direction unless acted upon by an unbalanced force.' The battering ram, consisting of a heavy longitudinal object, is put in directed motion by human and/or mechnical means, with the ram maintaining its direction and speed until prevented doing so by the object it strikes – in this case a fortress wall or gate.

As it strikes the surface, that surface has to be strong enough to resist the inertia of the ram's impact – if it isn't, then it wholly or partially collapses. Newton's Second Law of Motion also comes into play, summarised in the equation $F=ma$. 'The force (F) acting on an object is equal to the mass (m) of an object times its acceleration (a).' By this law, the heavier the battering ram the more power is required to put it in motion, but also the greater the force it delivers against a resistant object.

The theoretical physics behind the battering ram might not have been fleshed out during the ancient and medieval periods, but they were well understood in practice. A substantial battering ram, even a hand-carried one wielded by the heaviest men of the siege army, could eventually yield a breach, when applied with force against a weak point in a wall or door.

Yet, as so often in the world of siege warfare, the gulf between theory and practice could be profound. First, the defenders, ever mindful that force and motion would be applied against their defences, built walls of monstrous thickness to resist such efforts, as we saw in the previous chapter. This did not make such surfaces invulnerable, but what it did was to extend the time required to achieve

◄ *A sheltered battering ram, with the ram dismounted from its support ropes. A device of this size would probably have been operated by four to eight men. (Klearchos Kapoutsis/ CC BY 2.0)*

▼ *The earliest battering rams would have been wielded by human muscle. Even with rope grips, much of the power would have been lost in recoil in the arms of holders. (PD)*

▲ Two varieties of battering ram are in operation here, one hand held with a metal impact head, and one with a two-beam swing frame but wooden impact head. (PD)

▼ A reconstructed battering ram sits within the walls of Beckov Castle, in western Slovakia. Its high stone walls built on steep cliffs meant it was one of the few castles to withstand the attacks of Turkish troops in the 14th century.

▲ This reconstruction of a wheeled battering ram shows the basic A-frame system of suspension. Note how the ram beam is inclined relative to the frame. (Piotrus/CC BY-SA 3.0)

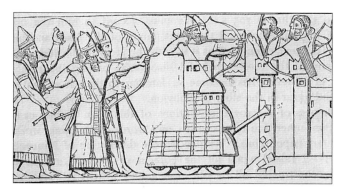

▲ *This image from ancient Assyria shows a battering ram built into a mobile siege tower. The upper levels of the tower serves as a platform for archers. (PD)*

a breach. And in the cruel attrition of a siege, each side's handling of time could make all the difference between victory and defeat. Every minute that the operators of a ram spent at the bottom of a wall, dutifully hammering away at the surface, was another minute they spent exposed to the defenders' attempts to stop them, the techniques of which we shall study below.

So, in the escalating logic of siege warfare, by creating a heavier ram capable of delivering even greater impact on the wall with each stroke, the siege force could therefore create a breach in a shorter period of time, by reducing the number of impacts required to smash through. In opposition, however, was the fact that the heavier the ram, the more force was required to swing it; in any given minute, the lighter ram could deliver more impacts per minute than the heavier ram, but with reduced force compared to the fewer, more thunderous blows from the heavy ram.

Finding the right balance between weight, power, time and protection (for the ram operators) was the principal challenge for those who created and unleashed battering rams against

▶ *Another ancient Assyrian image of a mobile battering ram. Note the slope built up the city walls to enable the ram to ascend to its fighting position.(PD)*

▼ *The decorative head in the shape of a ram did not necessarily assist the efficiency of the device; pointed tips gave a more focused impact. (Clarinetlover/CC BY-SA 3.0)*

the enemy. On this basis alone, we see that however simple battering rams appear in principle, making them effective battlefield tools was a mechanically and tactically calculated business.

THE BASIC RAM

Battering rams are almost certainly one of the oldest forms of siege weapon, with evidence of their use dating back to the 3rd millennium BC in the warfare of the ancient Near East.

Hand held

At their most simple, battering rams consisted of nothing more than a heavy log with one end sharpened to a rough point. The log was carried and swung by the arms of equal numbers of men standing each side, possibly with the assistance of rope loops to give a better purchase on the weapon and to resist the effects of recoil from the bounceback. The power of such weapons was limited, both by the size of the ram and the strength of the men hauling it. Likely they would only have influence over light timber structures or thinner stone walls, possibly walls already weakened by the work of other siege engines.

Yet the advantage of these devices was that they could be deployed in large numbers, and quickly. In one of the reliefs snaking around Trajan's Column in Rome, a hand-held battering ram is clearly shown in the hands of barbarian Dacian forces attacking a Roman camp. This image indicates that manportable battering rams were in use at least until the 1st century AD and likely beyond, at least in the hands of the less technologically developed warrior societies. In the image, the head of the ram is reinforced with a metal ram's head, an adaptation that was common in battering rams of all sizes and levels of sophistication. The advantage of applying a metal head to the ram was naturally that it was not blunted, as in the case of exposed wood, with repeated strikes against a harder surface. In the action depicted, the metal head

ROMAN BATTERING RAM

The huge log of this Roman wheeled battering ram is suspended from a crossbeam set in a rectangular frame. The frame itself does not have any of the protective coverings of wood and hides. The height of the frame means that the suspension ropes are allowed a greater length. Longer ropes meant that the ram went through a greater swing, which in turn meant that the log gatherered extra momentum for a more powerful impact.

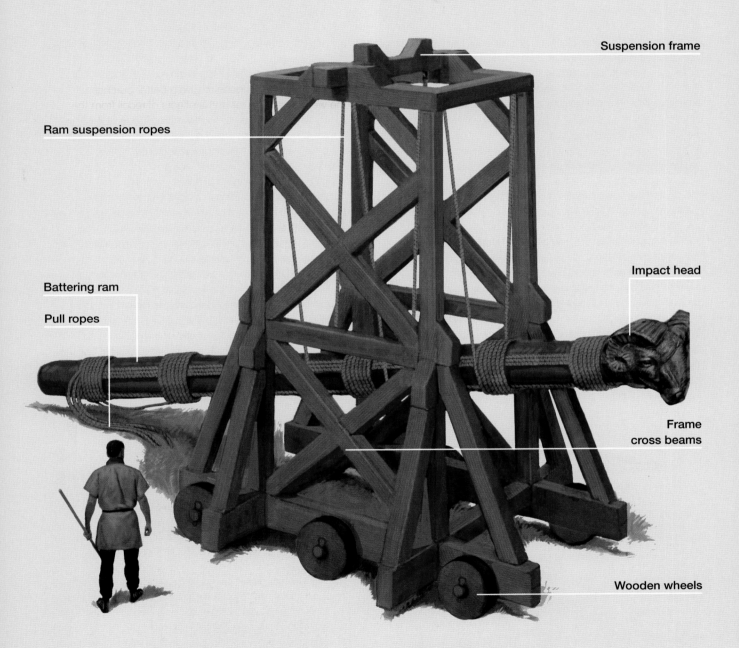

Suspension frame

Ram suspension ropes

Impact head

Battering ram

Pull ropes

Frame cross beams

Wooden wheels

▲ *A hand-held ram is deployed against a main door during the siege of Wilton Abbey by Robert of Gloucester in 1143. (Wolfgang Sauber/CC BY-SA 3.0)*

◄ *The short chain lengths of this reconstructed battering ram would mean a very short, but rapid, arc of swing. (Classiccardinal/CC BY-SA 4.0)*

would actually have been harder than the wooden camp palisade against which it was deployed.

The image of the hand-held battering ram on Trajan's Column immediately suggests the limitations of this man-powered device. Not only is the weapon necessarily light so that humans – in this case two men – can carry it with arm strength alone, but the image vividly depicts the attackers as being horribly exposed to the lethal hail of missiles from the defenders on the battlements; the Roman soldiers appear to be taking almost leisurely interest in who to hit with rocks. Thus it was that even as early as the 9th century BC, mechanical means and structural housings were applied to create more powerful rams that also provided some degree of protection for both the engine and for those operating it.

Protective cover and early mechanization

At some point in ancient history, siege engineers conceived of a simple way to improve the power of the battering ram. A heavy ram log, far heavier than human beings could physically carry, was suspended on chains or ropes within a rigid wooden housing, typically an A-frame. The frame was carried up to the fortress wall, and the ram was swung backwards by men pulling on attached ropes and handles, then released to swing forwards with assisted momentum to strike the wall. The advantage of this system was not merely that the ram could now be of very substantial size and weight, equivalent to that of the trunk of a large fully grown tree, but also that the ram could be positioned to strike the same point on the wall precisely and repeatedly.

The Roman engineer Vitruvius provides one of the earliest narratives for origins of the battering ram shed – or ram *tortoise* as it came to be known in the Greek and Roman worlds – in his 1st century BC work *De architectura*:

> It is related that the battering ram for sieges was originally invented as follows. The Carthaginians pitched their camp for the siege of Cadiz. They captured an outwork and attempted to destroy it. But having no iron implements for its destruction, they took a beam, and, raising it with their hands, and driving the end of it repeatedly against the top of the wall, they threw down the top courses of stones, and thus, step by step in regular order, they demolished the entire redoubt.

Afterwards a carpenter from Tyre, Bright by name and by

▼ *Square-frame battering rams were better able to control the lateral motion of the ram beam, by having wide points of anchorage for the supporting chains, but were more vulnerable to impact missiles dropped from above. (Joanbanjo/CC-BY-SA-4.0)*

▲ *A close-up of the Assyrian battering ram/siege engine. The panels of hide covering are apparent here, which help to protect the engine against fire attacks. (PD)*

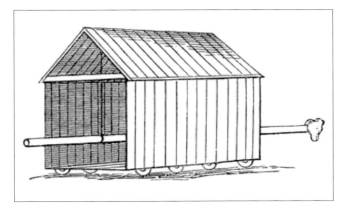

▲ *A simple ram-tortoise. The operators would stay inside the ram shelter to push it; the shelter had an open bottom for the soldiers to stand on the ground. (PD)*

nature, was led by this invention into setting up a mast from which he hung another crosswise like a steelyard, and so, by swinging it vigorously to and fro, he threw down the wall of Cadiz. Geras of Chalcedon was the first to make a wooden platform with wheels under it, upon which he constructed a framework of uprights and crosspieces, and within it he hung the ram, and covered it with oxhide for the better protection of the men who were stationed in the machine to batter the wall. As the machine made but slow progress, he first gave it the name of the tortoise of the ram.[1]

Vitruvius' account is correct in outline, but wrong in detail. In fact, ram engines of some considerable sophistication were already in operation by the 9th century BC. An Assyrian gypsum wall panel relief from the reign of Ashurnasirpal II (r. 883–58 BC) shows a six-wheeled covered shed, complete with elevated turret at the front as a fighting platform for archers, attacking the walls of a town with a large battering ram swinging out from the front of the engine, bringing down the mud-brick walls. Scale issues make the size of the engine open to interpretation, but the overall frame was possibly about 5m (16ft 5in) long and 3m (9ft 12in) high to its main transverse beam, with the total height of the turret about 6m (19ft 8in).

The tortoise

The crucial additions here were the wheels, which allowed the dead weight of the frame and the ram arm to be moved up to the enemy walls, and also the protective shelter to house the ram operators. The actual coverings of the ram shed changed little over time – typically a wicker or wooden lattice was covered with panels of rawhide, the latter as a fire-retardant measure. (A thick layer of clay was another measure against

▼ *The head of this replica battering ram features both impact point and hook, the latter would claw away at crumbling masonry when the ram was retracted. (Sandstein/CC BY 3.0)*

RAM WITH TORTOISE

Battering rams rely on a repeated pendulum action to deliver their impact against the surface. The longer the suspension ropes, the longer the operators could apply acceleration and power throughout the swing, and the greater the momentum built up behind the ram under its own weight.

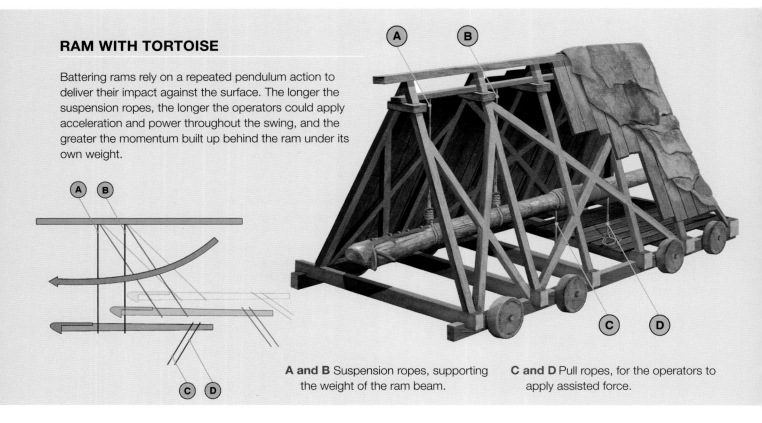

A and B Suspension ropes, supporting the weight of the ram beam.

C and D Pull ropes, for the operators to apply assisted force.

fire.) Ram-shed roofs also tended to be angled in a gable-end design to deflect the downward blows of rocks and other missiles dropped from the battlements. These mobile shelters were classically known as *tortoises*, a term then was applied to any mobile shed protecting soldiers or siege engines, not just battering rams. The ram-tortoises were a recognition that

the weakest link – i.e. the most vulnerable – in the system was the human operators. During the Roman period, we even see evidence of two-stage ram tortoises in operation; the first, larger tortoise held the ram machinery and was followed by a second, smaller mobile shed that provided a sheltered operating space for the attendant warriors.

▶ *An illustration of a ram-tortoise from Athenaeus Mechanicus' work on siege craft. Note how the shelter is actually below the ram in this layout. (PD)*

▼ *The rear of a ram-tortoise. Nearby soldiers would have to give the ram a wide berth when it was moving, to avoid the lethal beam as it swung out the back. (Ballista/CC BY 3.0)*

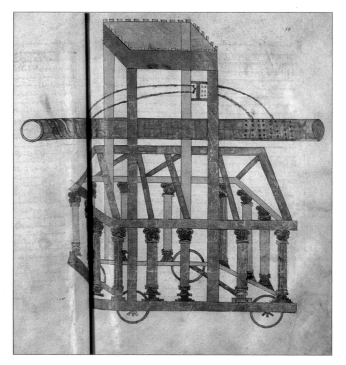

A British 19th-century vision of a Roman battering ram. The team stand behind the beam, drawing it back over their heads before sling-shotting it forward. (PD)

SIEGE TACTICS: RAM POSITIONING

Utilising a battering ram effectively was not simply a matter of wheeling it up to a wall and banging away. The location of attack had to be chosen carefully. Rams were best applied to thinner sections of wall, angles where two walls joined one another, or to parts already damaged by other attacks. In terms of the precise positioning, the ram head was ideally directed against the mortar holding stone slabs together, not at the stone slabs themselves, as this gave the most efficient likelihood of forming a breach and not damaging the ram head, ram body or the frame of the tortoise.

There was also the issue of the height of attack. Remember, the purpose of the battering ram was not entirely that of bringing down a whole section of wall, although this was useful if it occurred, but rather to create a hole through which soldiers could pass through. (Modern experiments with reconstructed rams and fortress walls have shown that creating even a sizeable hole in the wall face often does not result in a total collapse of the structure above; furthermore, once a ram has punched a

hole through, the head will then swing uselessly through the hole unless the whole engine is repositioned.) Height positioning of the ram was therefore crucial: too low, and the ram would have to negotiate what was typically the thickest part of the wall, often flared out in a *talus* to defeat undermining; too high, and the follow-up assault force might struggle to perform the escalade or climb up to the breach height. Yet, on some occasions, towering siege engines with rams mounted several stories up were applied to attack upper battlements, smashing the wallwalk and crenellation.

Often, to gain the right ram positioning, and also to help negotiate the wheel-wrecking battlefield terrain, an assault slope might be built up to the fortress wall prior to deploying the ram. Once in position, ram tortoises had to be firmly held in place if they were not to rebound under the recoil of their own impact. The wheels would have chocks placed behind them to prevent roll-back, although periodically the operators would likely have to shove the whole contraption forwards again to keep it in contact with the wall surface.

◄ *Note how the ram emerges at a steep upward angle from its tortoise. Ram beams were set either pointed slightly upwards or parallel to the ground, never pointing downwards. (PD)*

ENGINEERING ADVANCES

Sophisticated ram-tortoises were the mainstays of ancient warfare from archaic times to the end of the Roman Empire. During the later years of these periods, some of the principles and formulae for the construction of effective rams were laid down in engineering documents, many of which have survived through to this day.

SIZE AND SWING

From the Greeks, the names of military engineers Polydius, Diades and Charias stand out, principally because of their design of ram-tortoises to support the imperial campaigns of Philip II of Macedon and his son Alexander in the 4th century BC. Thucydides also gives an account of battering rams being used against the Plataeans during the Peloponnesian War (431–404 BC). What is apparent is that ram-tortoises were scaling up in their dimensions and force. The enlargement of the rams had a certain logic to it. The most powerful ram beams were not only heavy, and therefore required large structures to deploy them, but to deliver the most impact they had to have a long arc of swing. That meant heightening the roof of the ram shelter to lengthen the suspension cables, sufficient to give the ram its maximum effective swing. Vitruvius explains how during the 4th century BC, Diades and Charias produced a standardised series of tortoises, of different sizes to match the challenge they faced. One of the most sizeable specimens is described as follows, related in dimensions to mighty siege towers.

> He [Diades] also employed the ram mounted on wheels, an account of which he left in his writings. ...
>
> The tortoise of the battering ram ... had a base of thirty cubits [13.7m] square, and a height, excluding the pediment, of thirteen cubits [5.9m]; the height of the pediment from its bed to its top was seven cubits [3.2m]. Issuing up and above the middle of the roof for not less than two cubits [90cm] was a gable, and on this was reared a small tower four stories high, in which, on the top floor, *scorpiones* [small arrow-firing catapults] and catapults were set up, and on the lower floors a great quantity of water was stored, to put out any fire that might be thrown on the tortoise. Inside of this was set the machinery of the ram, ... in which was placed a roller, turned on a lathe, and the ram, being set on top of this, produced its great effects when swung to and fro by means of ropes. It was protected, like the tower, with rawhide.[2]

Many points jump out from this account. The first is that the ram is incorporated into a towering multi-weapon mobile platform, which not only incorporated several different types of ballistic weapons on its floors – useful for suppressing the fire of defenders while the ram team was at work – but which also included its very own fire-extinguisher system. Note also the penultimate sentence, which describes the use of a roller

to assist the ram movement. There has been some historical confusion about what this actually means. Arguably the likeliest configuration is that the ram ran over a roller at the front of its travel, to control its direction and accuracy on the swing, with the motive power still coming from men pulling on ropes behind it.

HEGETOR'S TORTOISE

Diades' ram-tortoise was not the biggest specimen in the ancient world. That accolade seems to go (according to Vitruvius) to one Hegetor of Byzantium, who created an eight-wheel monster that weighed more than 150 tonnes and was operated by over 100 men.

▼ *When set in towers, rams could be positiioned either at the bottom for pounding the wall's foundations or at the top for attacking parapets. (Lifestyle pictures/Alamy)*

TIME AND TACTICAL CONSIDERATIONS

We have already seen how critical positioning was to the efficacy of a ram weapon (p.47); the military commander had to 'read' the fortress to ascertain the best place (i.e. the weakest spot or that most advantageous for follow-up assault) and the best height at which to make the attack. This choice became harder as fortress design itself began to respond, during the ancient period, to the application of battering rams. For example, many ancient towns and cities had what are known as 'casemate walls', which consisted of two relatively thin parallel outer walls, the space between them used for storage and also habitation. Because the individual walls were relatively thin, they could be breached easily by battering rams, hence solid and deep stone structures became more common, especially for important or capital cities. These took time and commitment to breach.

Indeed, one of the most important tactical factors in the deployment of a battering ram was *time* itself. For a start, there was the time it took to transport or manufacture a battering ram. Rams were rarely moved for miles on their own wheels (if they were of the wheeled variety), but rather the components were transported by animal-drawn cart, river boat or ship to their destination, where the ram was assembled. Alternatively, the ram might be built from scratch at the site of the siege, if the commander felt that the siege wasn't going to be resolved any time soon and he could afford the several days of ram building. Thankfully, constructing a ram was not as complex a business as

▲ *This powerful recreation of the siege of Jerusalem in 1099 demonstrates the industrial levels of investment in engines and personnel to sustain a prolonged campaign. (Getty)*

manufacturing, say, a tall siege tower, but materials could be tricky to find. The ram beam itself, if it was to tackle a particularly thick wall, needed to be made from a single trunk of hardwood, such as oak or ash, with a uniform structure throughout to prevent it splitting from the repeated impacts. Finding a suitable piece of wood could be a challenge, especially in barren regions, but if a good piece could be sourced, a ram could be made in 1–3 days by proficient workers.

The biggest time factor behind the use of a battering ram was obviously the amount of hours and days it took to accomplish a breach. This period could be considerable. During the Roman siege of Jerusalem in 37 BC, it took more than two weeks of hammering away to punch through certain sections of the city defences. While such efforts were underway, of course, the attackers were not left alone to continue their work, but both ram and its operators would be under constant attack (see p.55 for defensive strategies). Thus the tactical use of battering rams also required the application of supporting troops and siege engines, providing a constant stream of suppressing fire against the countermeasures delivered from the battlements. The ram itself therefore became the centre of a connected tactical system, involving potentially hundreds of men in the combined effort to make a slender breach at a key point.

◄ *This reconstructed ram-tortoise has a protective shed built around the ram aperture, to protect the beam from boulders and hooks. (Ballista/CC BY-SA 3.0)*

Some historians have questioned the plausibility of Vitruvius' description, pointing out several impracticalities, such as the extreme length of the ram beam, which might have rendered it vulnerable to shattering. This is Vitruvius' account:

There is also another kind of tortoise, which [...] has around it boards, and eaves sloping downwards, and is covered with boards and hides firmly fastened in place. Above this let clay kneaded with hair be spread to such a thickness that fire cannot injure the machine. These machines can, if need be, have eight wheels, should it be necessary to modify them with reference to the nature of the ground. Tortoises, however, which are intended for excavating [...] have all the other details as described above, but their fronts are constructed like the angles of triangles, in order that when missiles are shot against them from a wall, they may receive the blows not squarely in front, but glancing from the sides, and those excavating within may be protected without danger.

It does not seem to me out of place to set forth the principles on which Hegetor of Byzantium constructed a tortoise. The length of its base was 63 feet [19.2m], the breadth 42 [12.8m]. The corner posts, four in number, which were set upon this framework, were made of two timbers each, and were 36 feet [10.9m] high, a foot and a quarter [40cm] thick, and a foot and a half [50cm] broad. The base had eight wheels by means of which it was moved about. The height of these wheels was six and three quarters feet [60cm], their thickness three feet [90cm]. Thus constructed of three pieces of wood, united by alternate opposite dovetails and bound together by cold-drawn iron plates, they revolved in the trees or *amaxopodes*.

Likewise, on the plane of the crossbeams above the base, were erected posts 18 feet [5.5m] high, three quarters of a foot [20cm] broad, two thirds of a foot thick [18cm], and a foot and three quarters apart; above these, framed beams, a foot broad and three quarters of a foot [50cm] thick, held the whole structure together; above this the rafters were raised, with an elevation of 12 feet [3.7m]; a beam set above the rafters united their joinings. They also had bridgings fastened transversely, and a flooring laid on them protected the parts beneath.

It had, moreover, a middle flooring on girts, where *scorpiones* and catapults were placed. There were set up, also, two framed uprights 45 feet [13.7m] long, a foot and a half [50cm] in thickness, and three quarters of a foot [20cm] in breadth, joined at the tops by a mortised crossbeam and by another, halfway up, mortised into the two shafts and tied in place by iron plates. Above this was set, between the shafts and the crossbeams, a block pierced on either side by sockets, and firmly fastened in place with clamps. In this block were two axles, turned on a lathe, and ropes fastened from them held the ram.

Over the head of these (ropes) which held the ram, was placed a parapet fitted out like a small tower, so that, without danger, two soldiers, standing in safety, could look out and report what the enemy were attempting. The entire

▶ *A series of variant ram-tortoise designs, from a 16th-century text. Note also the three-pronged ram head in the lowest artwork, like a fish spear. (PD)*

ram had a length of 180 feet [54.8m], a breadth at the base of a foot and a quarter [40cm], and a thickness of a foot [0.3m], tapering at the head to a breadth of a foot [30cm] and a thickness of three quarters of a foot [20cm].

This ram, moreover, had a beak of hard iron such as ships of war usually have, and from the beak iron plates, four in number, about 15 feet [4.6m] long, were fastened to the wood. From the head to the very heel of the beam were stretched cables, three in number and eight digits thick, fastened just as in a ship from stem to stern continuously, and these cables were bound with cross girdles a foot and a quarter apart. Over these the whole ram was wrapped with rawhide. The ends of the ropes from which the ram hung were made of fourfold chains of iron, and these chains were themselves wrapped in rawhide.

Likewise, the projecting end of the ram had a box framed and constructed of boards, in which was stretched a net made of rather large ropes, over the rough surfaces of which one easily reached the wall without the feet slipping. And this machine moved in six directions, forwards (and backwards), also to the right or left, and likewise it was elevated by extending it upwards and depressed by inclining it downwards. The machine could be elevated to a height sufficient to throw down a wall of about 100 feet [32m], and likewise in its thrust it covered a space from right to left of not less than 100 feet [32m]. One hundred men controlled it, though it had a weight of 4,000 talents, which is 480,000 pounds [217,725kg].'[3]

A. *Teſtudo ſimplex.*   B. *Roſtrata.*   C. *Arietaria.*

THE RAM DECLINES

The battering ram remained in use throughout the Middle Ages, during which it developed little from the time of the Greeks and the Romans. We hear of mobile rams being used heavily during the barbarian incursions into France and Western Europe (c. 300–700 AD), the Anglo-Saxon invasion of Britain (mid 5th to early 7th century), the Crusades and the various internecine dynastic, civil and territorial conflicts Europe found itself in throughout the medieval period. It was ultimately the rise of the cannon from the 14th century, however, that finally rendered the battering ram redundant. Cannon offered what the ram could not – stand-off distance, with potentially several hundred yards of relatively safe distance between the muzzle of the cannon and the wall it was firing at.

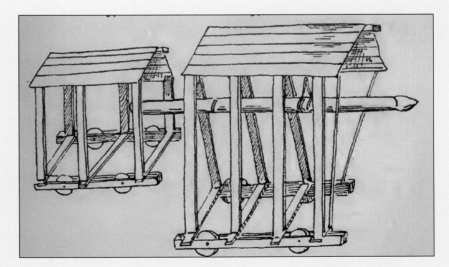

▲ *A 19th-century representation of two Roman four-wheeled mobile sheds, including one featuring a battering ram. (PD).*

BORING MACHINES

Called *tryanon* by the Greeks, and *terebra* by the Romans, the borer was, as its name suggests, essentially a rotational ram. Boring machines are far less common than rams in primary sources, appearing only rarely in illustrations and in a select few textual descriptions, principally Vitruvius' *De architectura*, Apollodorus' *Poliorcetica* and some Byzantine military manuals.

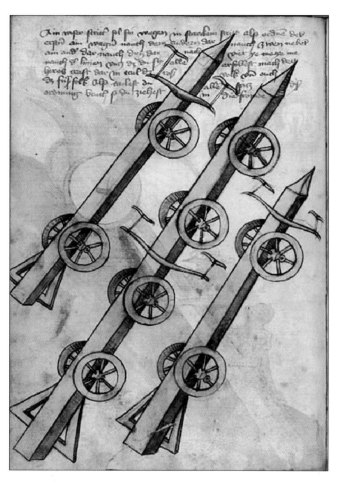

Unlike the ram, the borer was not designed to use impact energy to smash a breach through a wall, although some of the same principles of construction were applied to both ram and borer. Rather, the borer was designed to drill holes into defensive walls in a regimented pattern, with the holes creating a structural weakness within the structure that could be exploited. According to the ancient strategists, the correct application of the borer was to drill holes to a depth of at least 30cm (12in), placing the holes in a line about 90cm (36in) up from the base of the wall (to clear the thicker structures at the base) and each hole about 38cm (15in) from the next. Nossov notes that 'The holes in the wall were drilled upward at an acute angle to the wall, the idea being that the debris should empty out of the holes by itself while the borer rested firmly on the ground. Moreover, the inclination initiated the subsidence of the wall, as well as its falling in on the outside.'[4]

Holes in themselves would probably not be sufficient to weaken a major wall structure. So, after the holes had been drilled they were typically stuffed with wooden rods that had been soaked in pitch and sulphur to enhance their combustibility, then the rods were set on fire, with the fire weakening the wall structure further.

ROTATION TECHNIQUES

There are several descriptions of borer mechanisms. All share the features of a long shaft capped with a steel drilling head, with the shaft mechanically rotated to screw the drilling head into the wall. The biggest challenge was

▲ *A rather mechanically confused represetation of three boring machines by Hans Tolhoffer, from his work* Alte Armatur und Ringkunst *(1459). (PD)*

▼ *This drawing from* Athenaeus Mechanicus *shows a roller-powered boring machine, with the rotation applied from two rear winding handles. (PD)*

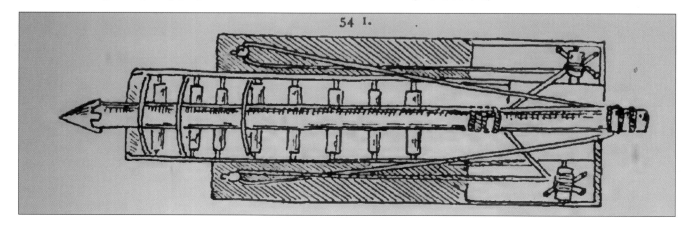

BORER WITH TORTOISE

Here we see the borer represented by *Athenaeus Mechanicus* (see opposite page, bottom) but mounted in a wheeled shelter, to enable the weapon to be moved up to the enemy wall while providing protection for the operators.

The operators would have turned the windlass handles, an action which would, via the ropes and pulleys, have imparted rotational force to the borer. The entire tortoise structure would have been covered in wet hides for fire protection.

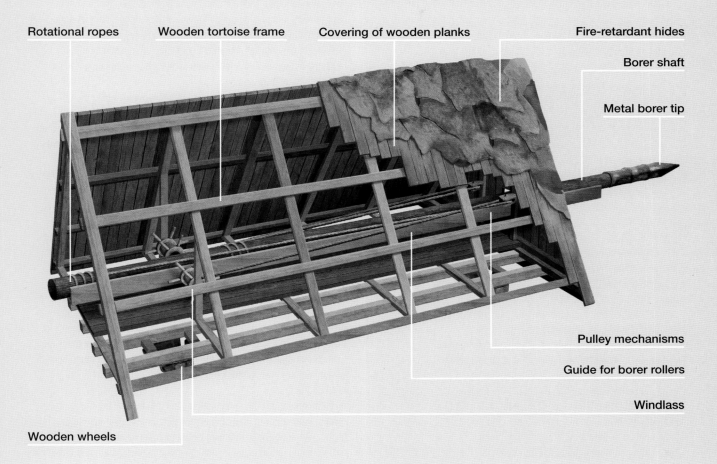

Rotational ropes

Wooden tortoise frame

Covering of wooden planks

Fire-retardant hides

Borer shaft

Metal borer tip

Pulley mechanisms

Guide for borer rollers

Windlass

Wooden wheels

BOW-DRILL BORER IN ACTION

The borer used here is of the bow-drill type, with the rotational force applied to the shaft by a tension cord twisted around it. By rotating the bow handle backwards and forwards, in the same way as a fire-starting bow drill, the drill bit was ground into the masonry surface. Typically the heads of such borers were very slender, only about as thick as a finger. The upward drilling angle allowed debris to fall clear.

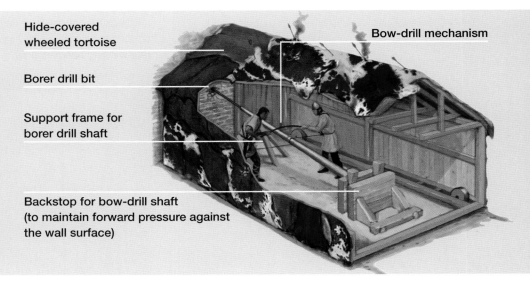

Hide-covered wheeled tortoise

Borer drill bit

Support frame for borer drill shaft

Bow-drill mechanism

Backstop for bow-drill shaft (to maintain forward pressure against the wall surface)

how to apply both rotational and forwards movement quickly, repeatedly and efficiently. Vitruvius explains the mechanical layout of one borer, developed by the ever-inventive Diades.

He [Diades] explained the principles of the borer as follows: that the machine itself resembled the tortoise, but that in the middle it had a pipe lying between upright walls, like the pipe usually found in catapults and ballistae, fifty cubits [22.8m] in length and one cubit [50cm] in height, in which a windlass was set transversely. On the right and left, at the end of the pipe, were two blocks, by means of which the iron-pointed beam, which lay in the pipe, was moved. There were numerous rollers enclosed in the pipe itself under the beam, which made its movements quicker and stronger. Numerous arches were erected along the pipe above the beam which was in it, to hold up the rawhide in which this machine was enveloped.

Extrapolating from this description, the borer tortoise was wheeled up to the fortress wall, and the drilling head positioned a short way from the surface. Soldiers operated the windlasses, which drove the 'pipe' (likely a solid log of wood with the drilling head inserted into a socket at the end) both forwards along the rollers while also rotating the pipe to create the drilling action.

Other descriptions of borers differ in the method of how the drilling head was rotated. Some have the drill turned by a bow-drill mechanism, with the string of a large bow mechanism twisted around the shaft of the drill; pulling the bow backwards and forwards therefore rotated the drill. (These drill types were actually common labouring tools, and would likely have simply been scaled-up versions for siege use.) Other diagrams appear to show direct-drive windlass designs, with the turning handle of the windlass seemingly geared directly into the drill.

Whatever the nature of the design, common sense tells us that borers had severe limitations. Critically, they would have been largely ineffective against fortifications built of solid stone, unless they could attack the mortar holding the stonework in place. For this reason, borers were better directed at fortresses made from either timber or brick, and consequently they do not appear frequently in Western European warfare, but more commonly in sieges in southern Europe and the Middle East.

◀ *Another rather confusing medieval representation of a boring engine with the support rollers showing as wheels. Note also the metal bracing around the wooden shaft. (PD)*

▼ *An 11th-century chronicle features an illustration of a simple bow-drill borer, with a diamond-shaped head ideal for grinding out the mortar between bricks. (PD).*

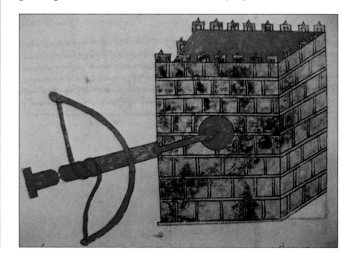

DEFENSIVE STRATEGIES

Battering ram attacks had to be dealt with as quickly as possible by the defenders. If the wall was not particularly stout, and the ram was of considerable weight and broad swing, then it might take little more than one or two dozen impacts before a significant breach was obtained, so time was of the essence.

▼ *In this Assyrian artwork, the head of the battering ram appears to have been hooked with chains, which two men are attempting to free. (Inglonghurst/CC BY-SA 3.0)*

▼*Three types of defence against a battering ram: a thick impact bag; a beam (designed to hook rams or sweep away ladders) and a swinging board. (Timewatch Images/Alamy)*

MISSILES

The default approach to tackling ram-tortoises, indeed any siege engine, was to pelt it with missiles of various kinds. Heavy rocks were dropped, not only in an attempt to smash the ram shelter, but also – if the timing was perfect and the aim spot on – to shatter the head of the ram as it contacted the wall; it was most vulnerable to being broken when it was at full extension. Fire and incendiary weapons were also unleashed against the rams. Although the protective materials on the siege engine, such as hides, metal sheets, clay and water-soaked fabric, went a long way to preventing fire taking hold, a constant saturation from fire arrows or incendiary grenades could indeed set a wood-framed tortoise ablaze.

HOOKING

Yet as well as the general defence against battering rams, there was also the particular. One distinctive counter-measure was to attempt to hook the head of the ram with rope nooses, or iron hooks dangling on the end of ropes, or fixed to the end of long poles. If the ram beam could be hooked and hoisted upwards, it could possibly be unseated from its mount and, more typically, dropped heavily to smash its suspension cords or break its frame. At the very least, if it could be hooked at several points, its power

▶ *A siege tortoise as depicted by Apollodorus of Damascus. The shelter had to be steeply angled to deflect the rain of rocks and other missiles. (PD)*

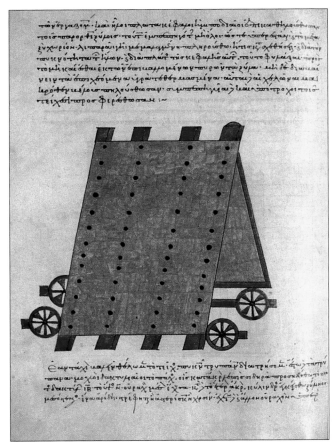

◀ *In this striking image, the defenders of a fortress are attacking battering rams with claws and rope nooses, attempting to lift up the ram then drop it down to smash it. (Getty)*

and functionality could be impeded; the defenders would unleash missiles on all those who ventured out to attempt to cut the snares. The hooking defence, with an innovation, is described by Thucydides in his description of the siege of Plataea in 429 BC:

> The Peloponnesians, together with the rising of their mound, brought to the city their engines of battery. One of which, by the help of the mount, they applied to the high wall, wherewith they much shook it and put the Plataeans into great fear. And others to other parts of the wall, which the Plataeans partly turned aside by casting ropes about them and partly with great beams, which, being hung in long iron chains by either end upon two other great beams jetting over and inclining from above the wall like two horns, they drew up to them athwart; and where the engine was about to light, slacking the chains and letting their hands go, they let fall with violence to break the beak of it.[5]

OTHER METHODS

Later in history, Vegetius extended the contemplation of counter-measures against battering rams to include a consideration of appropriate responses should the attackers manage to make a breakthrough.

> **Mattresses, nooses, grapnels and heavy columns are useful against rams.**
> Several methods are employed against rams and siege-hooks. Sometimes mattresses and packs of wool are suspended from the walls by ropes, to deaden the impact of the ram by the opposition of their soft and yielding material,

◀ *During the siege of Athens and Piraeus by the Romans in 87–86 BC, the Romans brought up siege towers and battering rams. Note here how the defenders have lowered a protective buffer down from the battlements, positioning this against the intended impact point for the ram. Bags could contain thick material but also rocks that might break the ram head on impact. (Hi-Story/Alamy)*

thus preventing the destruction of the wall. Sometimes the rams are caught by nooses, drawn upwards at an angle by a great number of men on the ramparts, and both ram and tortoise are overturned. A toothed iron instrument called the 'Wolf', like a pair of pincers, is often used; when lowered on ropes it seizes the ram and either overturns it or suspends it in such a manner as to prevent its striking the wall. Sometimes marble columns and their bases are thrown down from the walls with such force that they smash the rams to pieces. But eventually the violent strikes of the ram at last make a breach in the wall, which falls down. In this situation, the only recourse of the besieged is to demolish the houses, and build up another wall [using the materials obtained] inside the former wall. Then when the enemy attempts to storm the place, they meet their destruction on the ruins of the breach.[6]

Of note here is Vegetius' explanation of how padded materials could be used to blunt the impact of the ram head. Indeed, materials ranging from bags of wool to bales of hay could be dropped into the path of the striking point, taking the sting out of each blow made on the wall. The claw-like 'pincers' sound like an impressive tool for destroying a ram, or at least for controlling and limiting its swing. We must always bear in mind, however, that operating such a device would likely be a perilous business, as the men on the battlements would attract all manner of counterfire from the enemy below.

Rams, borers and similar weapons were the core tools in the arsenal of siege forces. As noted above, however, they were eventually replaced by the cannon, which provided that most welcome of qualities for any soldier – a safe (or less dangerous at least) distance. Yet as we shall see in the next two chapters, even before the advent of the cannon, besieging armies had a range of missile weapons at their disposal, some of which rivalled the cannon for power and reach.

▲ A 16th-century woodcut shows a variety of ram-tortoises, plus suspended-beam claw devices used for pulling down masonry. (World History Archive/Alamy)

◤ A variety of battering rams in action. The image top left includes a tortoise with a ram positioned to attack the upper battlements. The other rams are largely hand-held but with a single point of support from a basic frame. (Deutsche Fotothek/PD)

◢ This battering-ram reconstuction, with its ornate ram's head, is seen in the town hall of San Severino, Italy. (Clarinetlover/CC BY-SA 3.0)

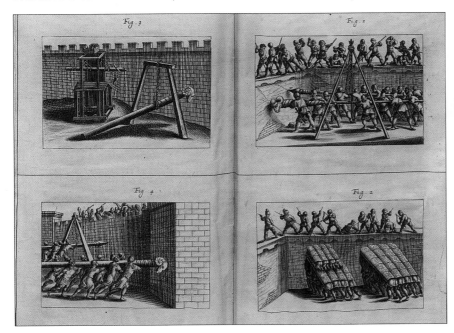

3

BOLTS AND BOULDERS: CATAPULTS AND TORSION ENGINES

In the thousands of years of human civilisation before the gunpowder age, artillery consisted of an array of mechanical devices for throwing bolts and boulders. Most of these worked via the spring-tension of bent wood or metal, or the force stored in a heavy torsion springs.

◄ *An artist's impression of Roman troops utilising torsion artillery to hurl stone balls against enemy walls. The balls would have been shaped and graded in an early system of standardised calibres. (Getty)*

THE MECHANICAL BOW

Catapults, whether bolt-throwing or stone, were the light and medium artillery of their day. Archaeological evidence and modern reconstructions show that some of these weapon systems were capable of precision fire over several hundred metres.

▲ *Human skeletons from Iron Age Dorset, have revealed, in some cases, death by Roman ballista bolt, fired during the Roman invasion of 43 AD. (Greg Balfour Evans/Alamy)*

▲ *A Roman-era relief shows an iron-framed cheiroballista, the metal torsion-spring housings clearly visible, mounted to a small horse-drawn cart. (Conrad Cichorius/PD)*

After the club and spear, the bow is possibly humanity's most ancient weapon. Its origins lie somewhere back in the late Stone Age, some 50,000 years ago, attested to by evocative cave paintings. While the bow and arrow certainly originated as a hunting tool, enabling warriors to tackle potentially violent prey from many metres of distance rather than at perilous arm's length, it is certain that its applications in fighting people would have been immediately appreciable.

During the 2nd and 1st millennia BC, accounts and images of sieges appear, at first in fragments but growing to numerous sustained narratives. The bow features heavily in these records, and would do so until the late Middle Ages when hand-held firearms eventually established their dominance.

THE MILITARY BOW

The humble hand-held bow might seem a rather impotent weapon in siege warfare, given the lightweight arrow's inability to penetrate stone and thick wood. Yet through the long history of siege warfare, the bow and arrow made a critical contribution. The primary function of the military bow was to inflict attrition and to impose suppression at distance. High-quality bows were capable of firing out to ranges of more than 200m (220yds) – tests with reconstructed English longbows were able to send arrows out to 315m (344yds) – and in well-trained hands such shots could be delivered with impressive accuracy. So, using bows, both attackers and defenders would be able to fire upon point targets of individual human dimensions, or upon small groups at longer ranges. And they could do it in volume. While users of the early gunpowder 'handgonnes' or muskets were lucky if they could fire more

than two or three shots a minute, none of which would be particularly accurate, and with an effective range limited to about 50m (55yds), a competent archer could fire six to ten arrows per minute (depending on the pull weight of the bow and availability of arrows) to 200m with a high degree of precision. Little wonder that bows were still in use around the world several hundred years after the invention of firearms.

THE GASTRAPHETES

As significant as bows and arrows undoubtedly were to siege warfare, they remained incapable of smashing heavy defences. In the early 4th century BC, therefore, military engineers surrounding the Mediterranean were turning their minds to developing missile weapons capable of leaving a more physically destructive impression. The first generation of these weapons was known as the *gastraphetes*, or 'belly bow' (for reasons soon explained).

It has been said that the *gastraphetes* was developed specifically for the defence of Syracuse against the warring Carthaginians in 399 BC, yet recent scholarship has deemed this a misinterpretation of Diodorus Siculus, who refers to *katapeltikon* (arrow-firing catapults) in 399 BC, these actually being influenced by earlier *gastraphetes*. Whatever the case, the *gastraphetes* looks to modern eyes rather like an oversized crossbow. Crossbows were indeed in use by this time in history, and had been so since the 6th century BC in

▶ *This reconstruction of an arrow thrower is basically a huge self-bow set horizontally in a frame, with the frame allowing for elevation adjustments. (AlexFilipov85/CC BY-SA 4.0)*

SIEGE TACTICS: PRECISION VS VOLUME FIRE

Of course, siege battles rarely involved archers working individually, although the arrow loops in many castles and fortresses attest to the selection of individual targets. There is more than one historical account of sieges being affected by single, sniper-like arrow shots. During the Franks' siege of Brissarthe, a Viking stronghold, in 866, for example, one of the Frankish leaders, Ranulf, was wounded by an arrow fired from one of the stone villa's windows, after which the siege was abandoned. Archers would also fire in volume, darkening the skies with clouds of missiles. For the attackers, heavy archery fire was an ideal way of suppressing the defenders' activity on the battlements, producing a covering fire under which escalade or sapping could be performed. The attackers could also lob arrows on a high arcing trajectory into the fortress interior, inflicting casualties on both soldiers and civilians and making free movement, so necessary to organising a defence, problematic.

Using the Franks again as an example, during the siege of Barcelona in 800–1, such was the volume of arrows flying into the city that it became almost impossible for the defenders to move across the battlements or the inner spaces of the city. Fire arrows, considered in more detail in Chapter 7, also raised the threat of a serious conflagration. Conversely, the defenders could fire their own barrages of anti-personnel arrows, doing so behind the fortress's excellent positions of cover and concealment. Fire arrows were used heavily against siege engines, and regular penetrating arrows put attacking infantry under a lethal fusillade that persisted from 200m (220yds) out to point-blank range. The main problem for those under siege was often that of ammunition supply – it was of course nearly impossible to retrieve arrows once fired over the wall, and difficult to manufacture new ones without large stocks of all the relevant materials.

◄ *A gastraphetes* being cocked. *The operator used his full body weight on the rear of the bow, which pushed the slider at the front backwards. (Selinous/CC BY-SA 3.0)*

various parts of the world. The *gastraphetes*, however, was more like a giant composite bow, but turned to the horizontal, mounted to a stock and fitted with a unique cocking system.

A composite bow is one made from multiple materials laminated together; the main body of the bow is hewn from wood as usual, but the belly is typically lined with horn, to increase compression under draw, while the face of the bow was covered with sinew, to develop greater elasticity when the bow was released. Composite bows produced heavier draw weights and faster releases than those made purely from one material, and were initially used to give mounted warriors or infantry shorter bows that could nevertheless command long distances. The *gastraphetes* was designed to deliver long-range, high-penetration fire over a range of about 200–250m (220–275yds), launching bolts of about 40–60cm (15–25yds) length from a pull weight of up to 90kg (200lb).

ROMAN MANUBALLISTA

Torsion adjusters

Bow frame

Torsion spring

Bow arm

Trigger

Elevation adjustment post

Frame

Cocking windlass

Slider

The torsion-powered *manuballista* was a key piece of artillery from around the 4th century BCE through to the end of the Middle Ages. Here we have a classic Roman design, the weapon mounted on a two-wheeled frame, the wheels provided the traverse while the adjustable piece beneath the slider provided the elevation. Two men would have typically operated such a weapon, which could have fired a heavy bolt as far as 400m (122ft).

▶ *A reconstruction of an ancient Greek* gastraphetes, *clearly showing the concave piece in which the bowman leant with his belly to cock the bow, and the ratchet cocking teeth on the slider.* (Haselburg-müller /CC BY-SA 3.0)

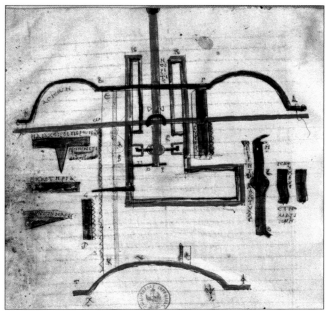

▲ *An illlumination from the work of Hero of Alexandria (1st century* AD*) shows an engineer's plan of a* gastraphetes, *with the recurve bow arm in green at the top.* (PD)

Cocking mechanism

Cocking such a heavy bow would have been impossible with simple arm-power, hence it had a mechanically assisted cocking method. The stock featured a semi-circular rest at the rear end, into which the operator rested his abdomen. The front end of the bow featured a slider mechanism attached to the main body of the stock and connected to the bow string. By leaning forwards with his full body weight on the bow, and with the slider placed on the ground, the slider and bow string could be pushed up the stock until the string engaged with the trigger claw. This held the string in position; a bolt was then placed in front of the slider and the weapon was aimed at the target, usually by placing it on a substantial rest. The weapon was then fired by pulling the trigger mechanism.

Mechanical refinements

The *gastraphetes* was the first in a developing line of large crossbow-like weapons, of increasing size and power. Zopyrus of Tarentum, according to the Greek historian Biton, developed two larger versions both known as 'mountain *gastraphetes*', one of which had a 1.5m (5ft 11in) stock and a 2.2m (7ft 3in) bow, and the other with a 2.2m stock (7ft 3in) and a 9m (29ft 6in) bow. These new weapons included some innovations that would have a shaping effect on future catapult-type weapons. The first was that a mechanical winch system at the rear of the weapons was fitted to draw back the bowstring, rather than the body-weight system. The second is that the engines were now fixed onto trestles or pedestals, with the larger weapon possibly including a swivel mount fitting for omni-directional aiming, although the exact construction of the mount has been the subject of ongoing debate. The larger device could even fire two bolts at one time, for something of an 'area effect'. What we have now is a crew-served direct-fire

weapon – essentially a type of basic artillery. The 'mountain *gastraphetes*' also came to be known as the *oxybeles* (lit. 'bolt shooter'). There also appears to have been versions of the *gastraphetes* adapted for launching stone balls of about 2.25kg (5lb), or 10–12cm (4–5in) in diameter, first developed by Charon of Magnesia and with a 3m (9ft 10in) stock.

▼ *An early* oxybeles *or* catapulta. *Note how the bow arm is clearly of a composite type, utilising horn and sinew to improve the elasticity.* (Arz/CC BY-SA 3.0)

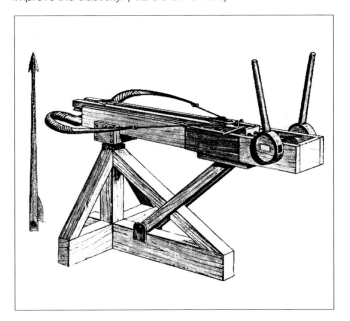

▲ *The ruined city walls and remains of artillery towers at Aigosthena, Greece. Catapults had 360-degrees of fire from the top of one of the towers. (Alamy)*

LIMITATIONS OF THE GASTRAPHETES

The useful point about these catapults for siege warfare was that though they were larger and more powerful than regular bows and crossbows, they were still small enough to be deployed from relatively confined spaces, such as towers and rooms. For example, a tower in the Athenian fort of Aigosthena, built c. 343 BC, had a top floor featuring three unusually large (for the time) window apertures on each side; it is believed that catapults were mounted behind each window for all-round firepower. Yet despite their convenience, the *gastraphetes* were in many ways little more than extra-muscular bows. They delivered heavy bolts to decent range, and had good penetration against wooden boarding, but they still had limited potential as anti-material weapons. Physical constraints in the design meant that more power could not be added simply by increasing the dimensions. Another power source had to be found.

TORSION ENGINES

The solution was the torsion weapon. In this design, which emerged around the middle of the 4th century BC, the unitary bow arm was replaced by two separate bow arms working together. The inner, thick end of each bow arm (known as the *pterna*) was inserted into a deep bundle of fibres (typically formed from a single length of hair or sinew cord looped around numerous times). The fibres were held between the arms of a wooden frame, passing through washers in the frame to engage with a torsion lever inserted through the end of the fibre bundle. The lever was then turned and locked, applying extreme tension to the fibre bundle to form a torsion spring, gripping the bow arm. (The engineers would test the tension of each fibre by plucking up and listening to whether it 'sang' musically.) Enormous mechanical energy was thereby stored in the torsion spring. When the bow arm was pulled back, it did so against this energy, releasing it when the trigger was pulled.

▼ *The trigger of a reconstructed Roman arrow-thrower. The knot held between the trigger teeth would have engaged a notch in the rear of the bolt. (MatthiasKabel/CC BY 3.0)*

Fire power and projectiles

What the torsion catapult provided was a revolution in both the power and the scale of siege artillery. The new weapons could launch substantial bolts out to ranges of 400m (440yds) and beyond, retaining massive penetrating force across the trajectory. Given the complex physical principles at work in the torsion artillery, however, much fine-tuning and mathematical consideration was required before the weapon began to approach optimal performance. The design of the frame, for example, needed to accommodate the powerful whipping effect of the bow arms. The torsion springs were held in vertical cylinders in the frame either side of the stock, and it was found necessary to shape out semi-circular sections at the rear of the frame to give space for the bow arms to lash forwards to their fullest extent.

There was also an optimal relationship between the diameter and height of the torsion spring and the length of the bolt to be fired. The general rule was that the torsion spring's height should be about 6.5 times its diameter, and that the diameter should be around one-ninth the length of the missile it fired. The role of the spring securing washers was crucial in this regard. The washers protected the wooden frame – in the days when the torsion lever simply sat on the wooden frame, the lever often became trapped against the woodwork and could no longer be adjusted. Numerous washer designs have been found, of many different sizes and configurations, especially in terms of how the washer locked into the frame and held the tension. The aperture of the washer also had a direct relation to the performance of the weapon and to almost all the other dimensions of design, as Duncan Campbell explains:

> Heron explains that the size of every component in the catapult was laid down as a multiple or a fraction of 'the diameter [*diametros*] of the hole which takes the spring'; or, in other words, the inner diameter of the washer. In short, the size of the washer was directly related to the overall size of the catapult. For example, a machine designed to fire an arrow three spans (69cm) in length had a *diametros* of four daktyls (69 ÷ 9 - 7.7cm), which thus became the basic unit of measurement for the entire catapult: the spring frame, being 6½ units wide (the length of the *peritrēta* [the cross pieces between the spring frames]) and 5½ units high (the height of the uprights plus the thickness of the two *peritrēta*), was 50cm × 42cm for this size of catapult; the wooden arms, at 7 units long, were 54cm; and so on.[1]

The formulae for designing the catapult became widely understood and applied from the 4th century BC until the decline of torsion engines in the late medieval period. The catapults were also mounted on three-legged pedestals, via a U-shaped bracket that allowed the 'gunner' some measure of fine-tuning when it came to accuracy.

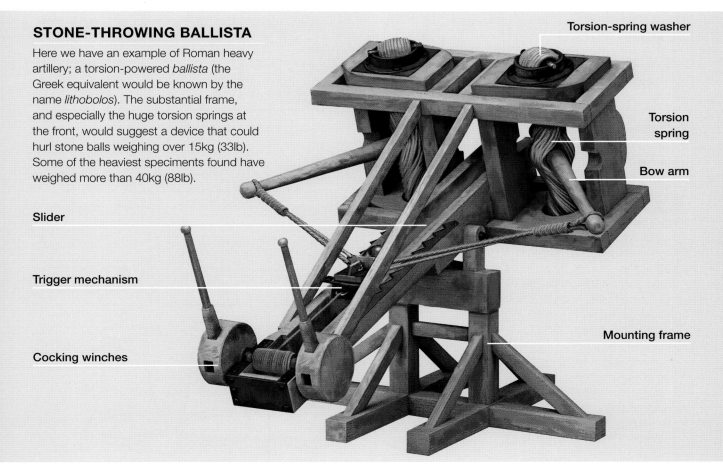

STONE-THROWING BALLISTA

Here we have an example of Roman heavy artillery; a torsion-powered *ballista* (the Greek equivalent would be known by the name *lithobolos*). The substantial frame, and especially the huge torsion springs at the front, would suggest a device that could hurl stone balls weighing over 15kg (33lb). Some of the heaviest speciments found have weighed more than 40kg (88lb).

Torsion-spring washer

Torsion spring

Bow arm

Slider

Trigger mechanism

Mounting frame

Cocking winches

(PSEUDO) HERON'S CHEIROBALLISTRA

One of the most detailed descriptions of an ancient catapult weapon is that ostensibly written by Heron of Alexandria (c. 10–70 AD), a mathematician and engineer. Weaponry was not the limit of Heron's ingenuity – other inventions included ancient vending machine, a wind-powered musical organ and theatre stage machinery. Yet an intriguing work entitled *Cheiroballistra* explains in detail how to construct a catapult weapon, such as was used during ancient and medieval warfare. It is important to note, however, that the text is actually unlikely to be from Heron himself, therefore the author is often referred to as 'Pseudo-Heron'.

The text describes how to construct a metal-framed torsion catapult, a fairly small one- or two-man device that would have primarily been used for anti-personnel fire during a siege, not anti-material effects. The detail of the text is exhaustive, providing exact measurements and step-by-step instructional guidance. To give a flavour of the text, here is part of the description of the trigger mechanism (NB: A dactyl was equivalent to the breadth of a finger):

And now we shall describe things related to the triggering mechanism. 'Let handle ABΓΔ be made(1) of wood as strong as iron (2), and of form such as has been drawn below. And the two-pronged component EZ shall have tenon EZHθ, which shall be rectangular. And the release mechanism [is] KΛM. And the little dragon [is] NΞ. And the pittarion [is] ΟΠΡΣ. And let a hole be made(1) to the handle ABΓΔ at Δ. And let a hole be made(1) to the beam EΔ, described earlier, at MNΞ, at MN with a round hole right through (2), and at Ξ with a hole that has parallel lines(3); and in this way let the handle be fitted, so that a pin pushed through(4) MN and through hole Δ of the handle unites them (5). And by perforating the two-pronged [component] Eθ at TY, and [by perforating] the release mechanism KΛM at Φ, and by pushing a pin through both holes TYΦ, we unite [them], so that the release mechanism can rotate around the pin unhindered.'[2]

Such detailed instructional guidance shows how the manufacture of siege engines became increasingly codified in the early centuries of the 1st millennium AD. Transferable design principles were essential to producing relatively standardised weapons, which in turn meant a higher degree of output in the manufacture of both catapult weapons and their ammunition. As a large besieging army might deploy literally dozens of catapult engines during a large-scale siege, conformity between individual weapons was advantageous to logistics and rates of fire.

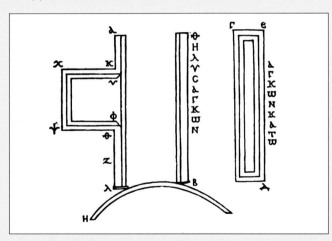

▲ *Diagrams of the case, slider (the track in which the arrow ran) and the 'crescent-shaped piece of the frame'. (Samuli.seppanen/CC)*

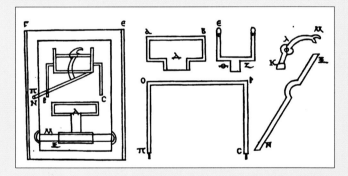

▲ *Instructions on the all-important trigger mechanism, which needed to be strong enough to restrain and control a bow cord under tons of pressure. (Samuli.seppanen/CC)*

▼ *The instructions for forming the torsion springs, with the four illustrations on the right showing the washer tensioning system. (Samuli.seppanen/CC)*

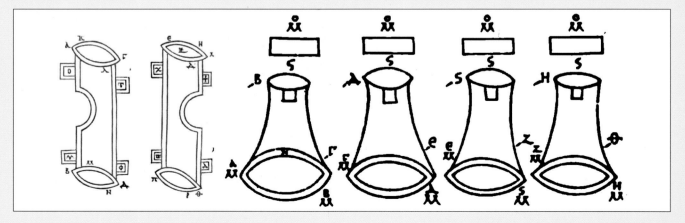

STONE THROWERS

In terms of anti-material devices, the new generations of torsion catapults were still limited in many ways by their bolt ammunition. Bolts can have impressive and ghastly penetrative effects against human beings, but if they strike a resistant surface – such as a stone curtain wall – the bolts often shatter, imparting only a small impact hole.

Early in the history of torsion catapults, therefore, we see an increasingly focus on adapting the technology to fire solid stone balls rather than bolts. Stone balls offered some advantages compared to bolts. They could deliver a greater impact on target through their weight, smashing masonry more effectively than bolts. Stone balls also tend to explode on impact, which produced something of a shrapnel effect, inflicting laceration and penetration injuries many metres from the point of impact. Stone was also very cheap and accessible for most armies, and a team of experienced stone masons could round off a block of stone into a serviceable ball relatively quickly, and without the exact precision processes required for the manufacture of quality arrows or bolts. Sometimes the ball might be coated in a smooth layer of clay to improve its aerodynamic qualities, but this was not an essential refinement.

ADAPTING THE MECHANISM

Stone projectors appear to have emerged during the campaigns of Alexander the Great in the 4th century BC. The physical structure of catapult-type engines needed some modification to handle the increased weight and very different physical shape and proportions of stones instead of bolts. Naturally the stock, slider and frame dimensions had to be altered, and many parts received additional strengthening. A pouch was fitted to the centre of the bowstring to cup the ball

▶ *The metal torsion-spring frame of an ancient Roman* ballista. *Metal frames were a revolutionary leap forward in torsion artillery, as they provided greater strength and functional consistency than wood. (Eunostos/CC BY-SA 4.0)*

▼ *A selection of the Roman* ballista *stones thrown at the siege of Masada in 73–74* AD. *The balls slung up against the elevated Jewish stronghold. (World History Archive/Alamy)*

▼ *An artistic reconstruction of a Hellenistic artillery tower, showing both stone-throwing and arrow-firing devices. (F. Kirschen/PD)*

▲ *A Roman reenactment team demonstrates use of the* ballista, *two men operate the cocking windlasses to draw back the bow string under tension. (Nick Turner/Alamy)*

securely throughout the launch. The power and length of bow recoil also needed enhancing, to cope with the extra weight and inertia of the stone ball. To do this, the frames holding the torsion springs were given a rhomboidal configuration, allowing the springs to be offset in relation to one another. The effect of this measure was that whereas the bow arms

▼ *Bolt-throwing (left) and stone-throwing* ballistae *juxtaposed. The stone-throwing engines required good clearance between the frame and the slider. (North Wind/Alamy)*

in the standard square-framed springs had a recoil arc of 35 degrees, now the catapult could exert 50 degrees of recoil arc on the stone. Also, the mathematical formulae for calculating the diameter and length of the torsion springs relative to the projectile were slightly different for stone throwers as compared to arrow throwers, although these formulae had been cracked by the mid 3rd century AD.

ALEXANDER AND THE SIEGE OF TYRE

Although, as we shall see, the nomenclature of bolt- and arrow-firing siege engines can be confusing, the new stone-throwing engines were called *lithobolos* by the Greeks and *ballista* by the Romans; small versions of these engines were known in Roman terminology as *scorpions*. The stone-throwing catapults quickly became weapons to be feared by any fortress garrison. Some of the beefiest examples were capable of launching stones 3 talents – 78kg (172lb) – in weight, with such missiles pulverizing rock and timber on impact. Available evidence suggests the first use of the weapons in siege warfare was in Alexander's attack on Tyre in 332 BC. The Macedonian commander, trying his hand at siege warfare for the first time, deployed and/or built numerous powerful *lithobolos* for the attack on the island city. Equally innovative was his application of the weapons – *lithobolos* were placed on ships to deliver an offshore bombardment, and also in mighty siege towers for close-range fire against the defenders. Eventually the might of the siege engines, plus the persistence of his assault troops, paid off and Alexander took Tyre.

INNOVATION AND CONTINUITY

The stone-throwing engines, and their bolt-throwing cousins, were centrepieces of Greek, Roman and Byzantine warfare until the downfall of their empires or states. In essence, they were the artillery of the ancient world.

Much like modern propellant-based artillery systems, there was some standardisation applied to both engines and projectiles. For example, the many stone balls found in various locations around the Mediterranean – 5,600 have been discovered at the former site of Carthage alone – have shown that the ancients had a number of agreed calibres, rising from weights of just 4.4kg (9lb 11oz) through to wall-shattering stones of nearly 40kg (90lb). Markings chiselled into the stones indicated their weight, much in the same way that we see calibre information stamped on the head of a modern shell case.

Some innovations were little more than curiosities. According to Philo of Byzantium, in the 3rd century BC Dionysius of Alexandria invented the *polybolos*, a magazine-fed semi-automatic bolt firer (to use modern terminology). When the operator turned the weapon's windlass handle, it set in train mechanical events that not only fed, via a cam-controlled revolving drum, one bolt at a time into the firing groove from a vertical magazine, but it also cocked the string and fired the weapon. All the operator had to do was keep turning the handle to cycle through the magazine. As interesting as this sounds, however, the *polybolos* was weak on power, and did not achieve widespread battlefield use.

REFINING THE TORSION SPRING

More important changes came about when Roman engineers looked again at the torsion spring system, in the 1st century BC. One of the chief problems of the torsion spring was that it was significantly affected by the weather. Hot, dry weather kept the spring fibres tight and energised, but wet and cold weather weakened them, causing them to stretch and lose some of their essential elasticity. One measure was to encase the springs in metal containers to give a certain degree of weather proofing. Oval spring washers were also introduced,

▶ *A detail of a ballista bow arm slotting into a torsion spring. In Roman times, the thread was tensioned using a device called an* entonion *(stretcher). (MatthiasKabel/ CC-BY-SA-3.0)*

▼ *A close-up view of the trigger mechanism and its connection to the winding mechanism and ratchet stop of a* ballista. *(MatthiasKabel/CC-BY-SA-3.0)*

allowing the use of increased volume of spring fibres without changing the dimensions of the frame. Other, more mechanical, solutions were also tried, including replacing the springs altogether with compressible bronze plates, but none was really successful.

THE CHEIROBALLISTRA

A more important innovation occurred during the 1st century AD, when the Romans took the catapults to the next stage in their evolution. The invention, seen depicted on Trajan's Column, was the bolt-firing *cheiroballistra*, also known as the *manuballista*. Here the metal-supported wooden frames were replaced with pure iron frames, making the whole structure a little more resilient and less temperamental than the wooden versions. Note, however, that the iron-framed weapons were only used for firing bolts – stone-throwing was still the province of the wood-framed engines.

We also have a new addition to the ranks of siege artillery, the *onager*. (There are indications of similar weapons dating back to 200 BC, but the more detailed primary source

◄ *A reconstruction of an iron-framed* cheiroballistra. *The iron frame also contributed to make the overall weapon lighter and more manoeuvrable.*

ONAGER

The *onager* was a crude-looking device, but it was capable of both power and range. The throwing arm, when released under tension, was arrested by the pad fitted on the cross beam, which was filled with resistant materials such as chaff. In other designs, the arresting pad was set in a forward-sloping angle, to give the arm more distance of travel

Impact pad

Trigger mechanism

Throwing arm

Torsion spring

Beam sling

Frame

Winding mechanism for torsion spring

Winding mechanism for throwing arm

▲ *Roman soldiers ready a small* onager *for firing, with the weapon mounted on wheels for mobility. The ball weight would have been in the region of 2kg (4lb).*

▲ *This reconstruction of an* onager *has a spoon-like throwing arm; a beam-sling was actually standard. (Colin Palmer Photography/Alamy)*

references begin in the 2nd century AD.) The translation of the term – literally 'wild donkey' – pays some tribute to the kicking manner of its operation. The *onager* was a stone-throwing weapon, hurling projectiles in an upward arcing trajectory. The stones were launched from a single upward-rising arm, held in a wooden frame by a large horizontal torsion spring. The forwards part of the frame included a crossbeam fitted with an impact buffer, for the arm to strike against and stop when unleashed. The rear of the arm included a sling in which the stone sat when loaded; the whip-like action of the sling at the end of the arm's travel further added to the weapon's range and power. The *onager* was capable of a respectable performance. Manned by a team of eight men, it had a range that was below that of a *ballista*, but it was capable of firing some particularly heavy balls – 20–30kg (44–66lb) was normal, but there are specimens up to 80kg (175lb).[3]

Changing terminology

During the first centuries AD, the names used for catapult weapons underwent something of a confusing change, showing little regard to the orderly minds of future historians. *Ballista* came to be applied purely to bolt-throwing weapons, of which there were now some sub-variants. The *arcuballista* was essentially now the old *scorpion*; the *carroballista* was a *ballista* mounted on a two-wheeled cart, as a mobile platform; and there was the iron-framed *manuballista*. The *onager* was now called the *scorpion*.

Such weapons served the ancients well in siege warfare, providing both direct- and indirect-fire options. The *onagers* would be used for indirect fire, lobbing heavy stones over

or directly against fortress walls, or using them to demolish towers – or siege towers for that matter, if fired by the defenders. The *ballista*, and stone-throwing catapults, could provide more targeted fire. Defenders could use them to punch through opposing siege engines, and attackers could apply the heavy bolts to destroying upper-level defensive features, such as protective merlons or wooden hoardings.

▼ *The impact pad of an* onager *received very heavy blows. In the largest versions, a large earthen bank padded with filled sacks would have taken the impact. (Mim Friday/Alamy)*

CATAPULT ENGINES IN THE MEDIEVAL PERIOD

The extent to which torsion-type siege engines were used in the Middle Ages remains a subject of some debate. Beam-sling stone throwers, such as mangonels and trebuchets, are readily identifiable (see Chapter 4), but the waters surrounding catapults are muddy.

The sheer number of names applied to medieval siege engines form a catalogue of confusion, especially as the individual engines often either aren't explained clearly or consist of strange hybrids with questionable authenticity. We can be certain that forms of spring-powered engines were used, but perfectly categorising the various paterells, algarradas, fonevols, calabres, fundae and many other engines can be an exercise in futility.

▼ *The* ballista *at Warwick Castle in England is one of the largest reconstructed specimens in the world. Note the width of the slider for the stone ball. (Detail Heritage/Alamy)*

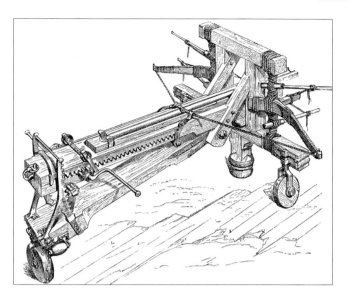

▲ *This sophisticated medieval cataput features caster wheels for complete freedom in lateral positioning, although they would likely need anchoring against recoil. (PD)*

▲ Ballista *bolt heads from the Somerset County Museum in Taunton, England. Such heads would have been capable of punching through plate armour. (Gaius Cornelius/PD)*

BELISARIUS

What we can certainly say is that medieval sources do make some clear references to catapult engines being used, particularly in the context of the wars of the Byzantine Empire and the Crusades. Procopius of Caesarea, writing in the 6th century AD, here speaks of the Roman general Belisarius' defence of Rome in 537, holding out against the Gothic hordes of Vittigis. In preparation for an assault against the city, Vittigis had constructed several impressive siege towers, but Belisarius was making his own preparations:

> But Belisarius placed upon the towers engines which they call *ballistae*. Now these engines have the form of a bow, but on the underside of them a grooved wooden shaft projects; this shaft is so fitted to the bow that it is free to move, and rests upon a straight iron bed. So when men wish to shoot at the enemy with this, they make the parts of the bow which form the ends bend torwards one another by means of a short rope fastened to them, and they place in the grooved shaft the arrow, which is about one half the length of the ordinary missiles which they shoot from bows, but about four times as wide. However, it does not have feathers of the usual sort attached to it, but by inserting thin pieces of wood in place of feathers, they give it in all respects the form of an arrow, making the point which they put on very large and in keeping with its thickness. And the men who stand on either side wind it up tight by means of certain appliances, and then the grooved shaft shoots forwards and stops, but the missile is discharged from the shaft, and with such force that it attains the distance of not less than two bow-shots, and that, when it hits a tree or a rock, it pierces it easily. Such is the engine which bears this name, being so called because it shoots with very great force. And they fixed other engines along the parapet of the wall adapted for throwing stones. Now these resemble slings and are called 'wild asses.'[4]

The description here shows that the *ballista* and *onager* continued as siege weapons beyond the last days of the (Western) Roman Empire, although we should note that his technical content is in large measure derived from the earlier work of Ammianus Marcellinus, the Roman soldier and historian of the 4th century AD. Some interesting details come from this account. Note, for example, that the range of the *ballista* was more than twice that of a conventional bow. Furthermore, the power of these engines on impact delivered both physical and psychological impact, as a later passage reveals:

> And at the Salarian Gate a Goth of goodly stature and a capable warrior, wearing a corselet and having a helmet on his head, a man who was of no mean station in the Gothic

▼ *This modern* ballista *shows a very early type of tensioning system, with the torsion adjusters sitting directly on the surface of the wood frame. (Scigeek/CC-BY-SA-3.0)*

◄ A ballista featured at Caerphilly Castle in Wales, reminding us that catapults were as much defensive as offensive weapons. (Detail Heritage/Alamy)

THE CRUSADES

We can jump forwards more than half a millennium and still find references to *ballistae* in action, showing some degree of continuity. The following is from a near-contemporary account of the siege of Ascalaon in 1153, when the forces of the Crusader Kingdom of Jerusalam under Baldwin III assaulted the Egyptian fortress:

> Finally, our men much strengthened in the Lord, committing themselves to the Lord with most devout prayers and making vows to the holy mother of God, attacked the wall on the third day; standing firm in faith, they moved forwards warlike implements, machines and ballistas. Truly, the True Cross went before the army in the hands of the patriarch. Then, indeed, by the manifest power of the Lord, all were struck by blindness, so that when a ballista by its force shot millstones into their midst, no one saw the incoming stone so he might move from the place and avoid the blow of the stone. Finally, hard pressed, they delivered the city into the hand of the king, and from that time Ascalon was made ours and possessed by our people.[6]

nation, refused to remain in the ranks with his comrades, but stood by a tree and kept shooting many missiles at the parapet. But this man by some chance was hit by a missile from an engine which was on a tower at his left. And passing through the corselet and the body of the man, the missile sank more than half its length into the tree, and pinning him to the spot where it entered the tree, it suspended him there a corpse. And when this was seen by the Goths they fell into great fear, and getting outside the range of missiles, they still remained in line, but no longer harassed those on the wall.'[5]

In this account, the *ballistae* are back in their earlier stone-throwing role, rather than firing bolts. The distinctions between bolt- and arrow-firing catapults do seem to be quite blurry within medieval manuscripts, and there are several illustrations that show both types of ammunition laid by the side of catapult weapons. For example, an illustration from Agostino Ramelli in 1588 presents an extraordinary three-armed giant crossbow weapon, incorporating two vertically strung crossbows and one horizontal crossbow. The weapon is likely a flight of fancy, but the presence of both bolt and stone ammunition in the artwork certainly indicates an awareness that catapults could be used for hurling both. What is interesting about the Ascalon account is that writer seems to suggest that such was the velocity of the incoming balls that the enemy don't see them until the moment of impact.

▼ Historical representations of siege engines can often lean towards the improbable, such as this multi-bow projector firing exploding or incendiary balls. (Alamy)

▶ The espringal, or springald, was a medieval variant of the bolt-throwing catapult, and appears to have been in use most prolifically during the 13th and the 14th centuries. (Konrad Kyeser/ PD)

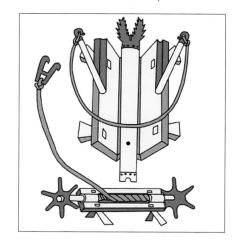

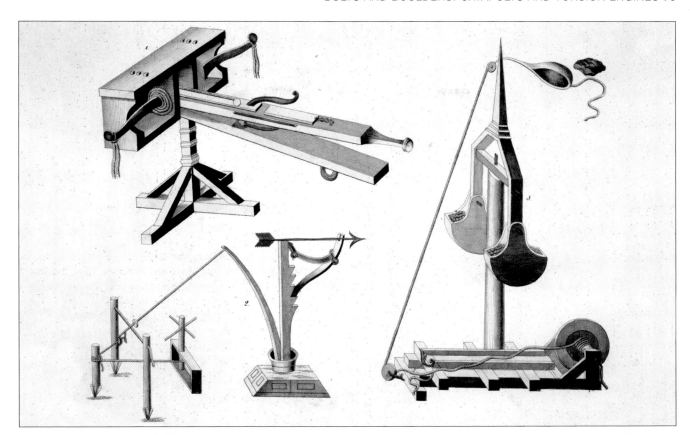

THE LATE MIDDLE AGES

Further accounts of spring and torsion engines are dotted around the later Medieval period, used in sundry conflicts from the Viking predations in Europe in the 8th century through to 14th-century battles in Spain.

In the 13th century appear references to a type of torsion engine, known by different names according to the country in which it appears, but commonly referred to today as the espringal or springald. This appears to have been a large torsion catapult, possibly with inward swinging arms, set in box-like wooden frame that measured about 2m (6ft 7in) long, 1.5m (5ft) wide and 1.5m (5ft) high. It was by all accounts a respectably powerful weapon, the animal-hair torsion springs collecting up to 1,800kg (3,970lb) of stored energy. These were bolt-firing weapons, and what bolts indeed – they were up to 80cm (30in) long and had an unusually robust shaft, 4.5cm (2in) in diameter. The total weight of the bolt would be in the region of 1.5kg (3lb), and their penetrative effect at velocity must have been enormous, punching through armour and shields with little difficulty.[7]

THE DECLINE OF THE TORSION ENGINE

A lack of clarity in the sources does not mean that we should airbrush torsion engines out from the sieges of the Middle Ages. Torsion weapons were indeed complex and sophisticated weapons to construct, but then again so were trebuchets, and they were prolific in the sieges of the Middle Ages. Enough references to torsion-type weapons are included to ensure their continuing service during the

▲ *Various siege weapons improbably conceived by Friedrich Martin von Reibisch in 1842, who completely misinterprets the* ballista *torsion-spring system. (Heritage/Alamy)*

medieval era. Yet the rise of the trebuchet from the mid 6th century AD, with its undoubted wall-smashing properties and more reliable performance in variable weather conditions, plus the advent of gunpowder weaponry in the 14th century, did make the decline and eventual disappearance of large torsion weapons inevitable.

▼ *If it were operational, the Warwick Castle* ballista *would likely have a range of up to 150m (160yds), depending on the elevation. (Ronald Preuß/CC BY-SA 2.0)*

HIGH-TRAJECTORY FIRE: THE AGE OF THE TREBUCHET

Traction and counterweight trebuchets dominated the landscape of medieval siege warfare. The biggest specimens were capable of throwing stones weighing 100kg (220lb) over 200m (220yds), smashing masonry and fortress buildings with repeatable accuracy.

◄ *Dover Castle siege, 1216. French forces under Prince Louis 'the Lion' used trebuchets (although possibly more of the traction type) to bombard the fortress. (Getty)*

TRACTION TREBUCHETS

Until the advent of the huge gunpowder bombards in the 14th and 15th centuries, the most potent of all the forms of siege artillery were the counterweight engines. Hurling stone balls weighing, in some case, hundreds of kilograms, plus many other types of missile, they were a terror to defenders attempting to preserve the integrity of their walls and towers.

In the previous chapter, we took an historical and technological journey through the many forms of spring and torsion artillery. Given their endurance across the centuries, these weapons doubtlessly performed with respectable reliability and effect. Yet there were problems at the heart of these technologies, not least that of durability under heavy use. Having already noted the issues caused by the effects of weather and climate, we can also acknowledge that torsion springs were mechanisms held under extreme pressures. Fibres within those springs could and did break, resulting in poor performance or repair downtime, and wooden frames were prone to fractures, warping and loosened joints from the incredible jolting forces unleashed whenever the weapons were fired. So, under the demands of a long siege, military engineers were frequently engaged in restorative work to bring the weapons back into working order.

The traction and counterweight siege engines that we will study in this chapter were not immune from malfunction either. Yet the very physical principles on which these devices operated were by their nature more robust and simpler. For this reason, they could be scaled up more easily, eventually hurling boulders of a size even the largest *ballista* or *onager* could not match. It was for this reason also that engines such as trebuchets endured in service until the 16th century, giving good accounts of themselves even by the side of the frequently temperamental cannon.

▶ *A 12th-century depiction of castle defenders using staff-sling weapons, throwing stones out from behind the wooden hoarding. (PD)*

THE SLING

In the hunt for the origins of the counterweight trebuchet, with some licence we can push our narrative as far back as the Upper Paleolithic period, 10,000–50,000 years ago. For it was during this era that the humble sling was invented, for both hunting and warfare. The sling consisted of nothing more than a long cord and stone pouch, but was a

▼ *A Persian manuscript illustration from the first half of the 14th century shows a counterweight trebuchet in action. (Granger Historical Picture Archive/Alamy)*

▼ *English staff-slingers attack a fortress from the sea during the Fifth Crusade (1213–21), using the weapon's high trajectory to reach the battlements. (PD)*

revolutionary technology for increasing the velocity and range of a stone throw. The cord physically extended the length of the thrower's arm, thus increasing the force of leverage, and when rotated quickly above the thrower's head the centripetal acceleration delivered tremendous kinetic energy to the projectile, doubling or tripling the range of the stone throw when the sling was finally released.

The sling continues to make a largely unchanged appearance even today, albeit principally in the hands of rioters and protesters. Yet another ancient evolution of the sling was the staff-sling, which possibly appeared about 170 BC in Macedonia.

Staff sling

This ancient and basic weapon consisted of a sling cord and pouch, attached to the end of a long stave. To use the weapon, a stone was placed in the pouch and the operator gripped the stave with an overhand grip, using both hands. He then brought the stave quickly up and over his head, with the stone being released from the pouch at the top of the swing, flying towards the target. The combination of arm and sling combined principles of leverage and acceleration to supply the range – principles that would later be directly applied to the traction and counterweight siege engines. The effective

▼ *Reconstructions of both traction (left) and counterweight trebuchets, the latter being of the fixed counterweight type. (Jebulon/CC0 1.0)*

range, based on some modern tests, was around 75–100m (82–110yds). (Think of the distance you can achieve with a modern plastic dog-ball thrower, which operates on similar but far less efficient principles.) The staff-sling was, in a sense, little more than a souped-up shepherd's sling, but with two crucial differences: 1) it could be used to throw heavier stones, on account of its two-handed grip and full use of the arms; 2) it did not require the many hours of practice required to become efficient with a regular sling.

Before we look at the emergence of related siege engines, it is worth acknowledging that the staff-sling was not just a battlefield weapon, but was also an extremely useful tool for siege fighting. There are several illustrations from the Middle Ages that show staff-slingers operating directly by the side of siege engines. (The medieval staff-sling was known as the fustibal.) Staff slings tended to be used to deliver bombardments of fist-sized stones against the defenders on the battlements, or conversely the attackers down below. Because of the arcing trajectory of the projectile, furthermore, the staff-slingers could also operate behind cover or walls if need be.

THE EASTERN TREBUCHET

Given the antiquity and applications of the staff-sling, it was only a matter of time before curious minds wondered if the same physical principles could be channelled into larger mechanical structures. The first steps were taken in China.

▼ A model of an early Chinese traction trebuchet. The key to an effective traction weapon was to ensure that the pullers were coordinated. (Gary Lee Todd/GNUFDL)

China

Although precision with dates is not possible, it appears that in the 5th and 4th centuries BC the traction trebuchet appeared in Chinese warfare. The earliest detailed description of the weapon comes from the writings of the Chinese philosopher Mo Zi. He described a four-footed wooden frame, standing about 4m (13ft) high. The two uppermost beams of the frame held pivot points, and between them was a pivot arm constructed from a cart wheel and axle. In turn, a long timber throwing arm was fitted to the pivot arm, this measuring a total of 10m (32ft 10in), with three-quarters of that length sitting above the pivot (when the arm was in its raised position). To the long end of the arm was attached a sling and pouch, while on the short end of the arm were numerous long pull-ropes.

This early traction trebuchet worked in the same essential way as all others that came after. With the throwing part of the arm lowered, the engine was aligned with the target and a stone or other missile was placed into the pouch (clay balls were popular, because of their fragmentation effects). Then a team of strong men, numbering in the dozens based on the size of the siege engine (some references give groups of more than 200 men), would take hold of the ropes at the opposite end, and on command would pull down on them with all their strength. This action would raise the throwing arm at speed, and at the top of its arc one end of the sling would detach, leaving the projectile to fly on to its target. The range of the shot depended on the force imparted to the ropes, so

▼ A 16th-century Islamic image showing the 'Catapulting of Ibrahim into the Fire' illustrates the principles of the traction trebuchet. (LACMA/PD)

the pulling teams likely had a set of commonly understood instructions for how hard they had to draw down. Maximum range of the traction trebuchet tended to be around 100–150m (110–165yds). Aiming was primarily a matter of aligning the device with the target, but for subtle directional changes the pullers could slightly change the placement of their feet and the angle on which they drew the ropes. These positional and directional changes were imparted to the sling-beam through the beam's natural flexibility. One particular type of engine, known as the 'whirlwind trebuchet', was actually nothing more than a beam-sling fitted to a single vertical pole driven into the ground and pulled down by just a handful of men. Given the physical limitations of the single pole in terms of stability, only lightweight stone missiles would have been fired from these, while the heavier stones were launched from the four-footed variation.

Mongolia and Japan

As historical accounts of East Asian warfare become more prolific in the Middle Ages, we see the traction trebuchet making regular contributions to the outcome of all manner of sieges, not only in China but also amongst the Mongols and later in Japan. Some particulars catch our attention. For example, it is apparent that traction trebuchets, in the hands of people who knew what they were doing, could be very accurate indeed, even targeting single individuals – enemy generals and their entourages were popular targets – and point positions.

For example, from September 1231 to January 1232, the city of Kuju (modern-day Kusong in North Korea) was besieged by the Mongols, led by their commander Sartaq. The Mongols had by this time heavily invested in siege-engine technology, including traction trebuchets, although so had the Chinese, and both sides traded missiles day and night. One of the Korean generals, Kim Kyong-son, was sitting defiantly on a chair on the battlements, doubtless affecting martial nonchalance while directing the fighting, and he came under direct trebuchet fire. One of the Mongol stones smashed into the wall directly behind him, killing many of his surrounding guards. Although Kim Kyong-son refused to move despite this encouragement, the incident demonstrated just how precisely the shot could be controlled. Other Mongol accounts speak of traction trebuchets accurately targeting individual ships as they approached fortresses, while some Japanese narratives of the 14th century speak of flag-bearers being consistently struck by trebuchet stones (although we always have to allow for coincidence as much as deliberate action). What is certain is that the trebuchets became integral tools of East Asian siegecraft.

THE TREBUCHET IN THE WEST

Just as occurred with gunpowder in the 14th century, so too did the technologies of the traction trebuchet move west into the Middle East and eventually Europe. The first appearance of these engines in the Middle East occur around the 6th century, as the Slavs and Avars (Eurasian nomads with strong Chinese influences) made incursions into the territories of the Byzantine Empire.

▲ *Trebuchet balls from the moat at Pevensey Castle, Sussex. The castle was bombarded by counterweight trebuchets in a 13th-century siege. (Manor Photography/Alamy)*

The Petrabole

The Byzantines called the traction trebuchets *petraboles*, which are described in the hands of the Avars by Archbishop John during the siege of Thessaloniki in 597:

> These *petraboles* were tetragonal and rested on broad bases, tapering to narrow extremities. Attached to them were thick cylinders well clad in iron at the ends, and there were nailed to them timbers like beams from a large house.

▼ *A modern trebuchet in the Schloss Veldenz, Germany, shows its capabilities. Note the unfolding of the sling at the top of the arm's travel. (Berthold Werner/GFDL)*

These timbers had slings from the back and from the front strong ropes by which, pulling down and releasing the sling, they propel the stones up high and with a large noise. . . . They also covered these tetragonal *petraboles* with boards on three sides so that those inside shooting them might not be wounded by arrows shot from the walls. And since one of these, with its boards, had been burned to a cinder by a flaming arrow, they carried away the machines. On the following day, they again brought these *petraboles* covered with freshly skinned hides.[1]

Here the Avars quite sensibly apply protective measures to their trebuchets, fitting boards to give some measure of cover to the trebuchet team and applying the standard fire-prevention measure of the day, covering the framework with fresh hides. The reference to the 'large noise' is evocative – trebuchets tend to make a distinctive whooshing sound when released.

The Byzantines became committed adopters of the *petraboles*, specialising in delivering heavy pre-assault bombardments. For example, a Byzantine army under Niketas pounded the Syrian fortress at Bikisra'il in 1032, killing some 200 of the garrison with their stones even before they surmounted the walls and took the castle.

The Manjaniq

The Arabs also embraced the trebuchet, which they called by various (frequently confusing) names, the most prominent of them being the *manjaniq*. The Arabs demonstrated impressive proficiency with the *manjaniq*. Historian David Nicolle, in his studies of medieval siege engines, has explained how the 'shooter' – the person controlling the placement of the rock in the pouch – could subtly control the accuracy of the trebuchet shot by fine-tuning the moment at which he released his hold on the pouch against the tension imparted by the pullers.[2] The investment in accuracy certainly seems to have paid some impressive dividends. In an account of the siege of Daybul, Pakistan, in 712, a large *manjaniq* was apparently used deliberately to smash down a flag pole that fluttered over the city, Nicolle noting that this 'remarkable shot so demoralised the garrison that the city soon fell.'[3]

The other achievement of the Arab military engineers was their realised ambition in scaling up the traction trebuchets in size and capability. The sling-beam, for example, was cut from a single huge piece of wood, in contrast to the Chinese practice of building up the arm in composite fashion from several overlaid planks or bound rods of bamboo. The Arab component carried with it great strength but also great weight, hence the *manjaniq* became ever larger, and therefore capable of hurling weightier stones with increased effect against masonry over ever greater distances. For example, it became perfectly viable to launch a rock weighing 60kg (130lb) for a distance of more than 130m (140yds).

Mangonel

Traction trebuchets, known both by the terms 'petrary' (amongst subtle variations) and 'mangonel', began taking hold in Western Europe during the 7th and 8th centuries, and quickly became a centrepiece of sieges throughout the continent and further east during the Crusades. Although it is the great counterweight trebuchets that tend to attract historical attention, it is clear that the traction trebuchets made a respectable and often fearsome contribution to the unfolding and conclusion of a siege. It is worth again quoting Nicolle to highlight this point:

> The way these man-powered siege engines were used can shed light on their power and effectiveness. They were often, if not always, used in batteries of several machines and at the French siege of Château Gaillard they were placed ahead of the French positions, presumably because of their limited range. During the siege of Lisbon in 1147 teams of 100 English Crusaders operated two machines in shifts, managing to throw no fewer than 5,000 rocks in 10 hours – roughly one every seven seconds. During a siege of Rouen in 1174 batteries of stone-throwers were operated by men working in eight-hour shifts. Even if the missiles were small, the moral impact of such a sustained bombardment must have been considerable and in 1145 the brand new castle of

Farington in England surrendered following such a prolonged bombardment, without the besiegers needing to make a general assault. A poem called 'Ercan li Rozier' by the French troubadour Bernat de Moncuc, written around 1212, suggests that even man-powered mangonels could damage a stone fortification: [...] 'I take pleasure in the archers near the loopholes when the stone-throwing machines shoot and the wall loses its parapet, and when the army increases its numbers and forms ordered ranks in many an orchard'.[4]

The continual fire of the traction trebuchets must have been wearying in the extreme for defenders. The heavy stone balls would have made light work on any wooden hoarding on the battlements, and would have readily smashed merlons. Thus, even if the defenders were not hit directly by the balls, they would have found themselves progressively stripped of their cover, on rubble-strewn battlements that became ever more complicated to negotiate. Yet, as impressive as the effects of the traction trebuchets were, they were eventually to be eclipsed by a new type of trebuchet, one that took the potential of beam-sling artillery to its absolute limit.

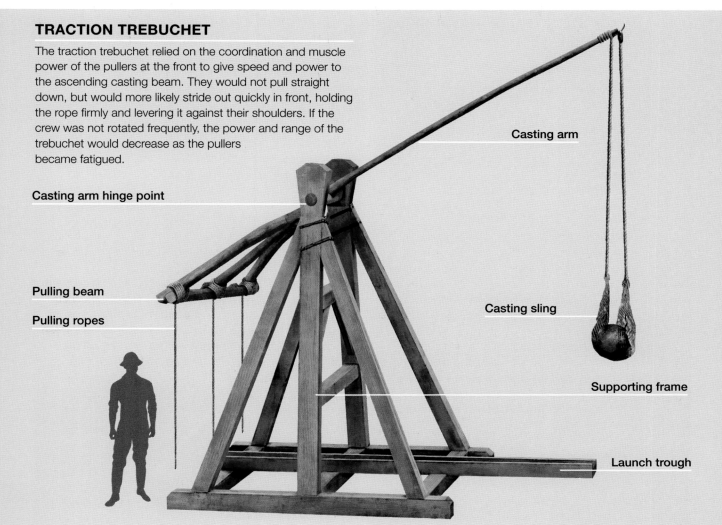

TRACTION TREBUCHET

The traction trebuchet relied on the coordination and muscle power of the pullers at the front to give speed and power to the ascending casting beam. They would not pull straight down, but would more likely stride out quickly in front, holding the rope firmly and levering it against their shoulders. If the crew was not rotated frequently, the power and range of the trebuchet would decrease as the pullers became fatigued.

Casting arm hinge point

Pulling beam

Pulling ropes

Casting arm

Casting sling

Supporting frame

Launch trough

THE SIEGE OF TERMES

The siege of Termes occurred in 1210, at the Château de Termes in the Aude *département* of France. The fortress, held by the Cathar heretic Ramon (Raymond) de Termes, was besieged for four months (August–November) by the French nobleman Simon de Montfort during the Albigensian Crusades. An early hope that Ramon would surrender because of a lack of water was dashed because of a sudden downpour of August rain, which replenished the château's water supplies. The description of the subsequent siege in the *Historia Albigensis* by contemporary Peter of les Vaux-de-Cernay contains some useful insight into the application of mangonels in siege warfare. Here he describes the tactical use of the mangonel once a frontal attack had failed. Note the defenders' counter-responses, which included return mangonel fire:

So the siege engines were set up close to the castrum and employed for some days in hurling missiles against the wall. As soon as our men saw that the outer wall had been weakened by the continuous bombardment of stones, they armed themselves with the intention of taking the outer bourg by a frontal attack. Our opponents observed this and as our men drew near to the wall set fire to the outer bourg and withdrew to a higher bourg. However, as soon as our men entered the outer bourg the enemy came out to meet them and quickly drove them out in flight.

▲ *The operator hanging from the ball could control, to a degree, trajectory and range of the ball by changing its release point. (PD)*

Such was the state of affairs when our men realized that their attempts to capture the castrum were being severely impeded by the tower of Termenet which I described above, and which was defended by a body of knights, and they

▼ *A closer view of the reconstructed* pierrière *at Château de Castelnaud, Dordogne, France. Note the hook trigger mechanism at the tip of the casting arm. (Jebulon/CC0 1.0)*

began to consider how they might capture it. They therefore set guards at the base of the tower (which, as I mentioned, was built on the summit of a high crag), so as to prevent the men in the tower having access to Termes itself or those in the castrum providing help to the tower if need arose. After a few days our men succeeded, with great difficulty and at great risk, in erecting a siege-engine of the type known as a 'mangonel' in an inaccessible place between Termes and the tower. [The 'tower' refers to a feature called the 'Termenet', a fortified tower built on a rocky crag just outside Termes itself.] The defenders in their turn erected a mangonel and bombarded our engine with huge stones, but could not knock it down. Thus our mangonel was able to continue bombarding the tower. The defenders now realized that they were besieged and could expect no help from their comrades in Termes, and one night in fear for their safety they sought protection in flight, leaving the tower empty. The guard at the base of the tower was being mounted by the sergeants of the Bishop of Chartres; they occupied the tower as soon as they saw what had happened, and erected the Bishop's standard on the roof.

Whilst this was going on, our petraries on another side of the castrum kept up a continuous bombardment of the walls. When our adversaries – who were admittedly courageous and astute – saw that the engines were weakening any part of the walls, they at once built a barrier of wood and stones inside at the weak point. The outcome was that whenever our men were able to force their way inside the walls at any place, the barrier built by the enemy prevented them from going any further. As space does not permit one to describe every detail of the siege, I shall simply say that every time the defenders lost any part of their wall they built another wall inside in the manner I have described.'[5]

The author goes on to describe how Simon de Montfort recognised that the sheer importance of the mangonel meant that it was vulnerable to a destructive infantry sortie by the defenders – no fewer than 305 men were therefore allocated to its protection. As predicted, one day a force of about 80 enemy soldiers rushed out from the fort and attacked the mangonel unit, followed by large numbers of other men carrying wood and lit torches, these men intending to set the siege engine on fire. A valiant defence by one knight in particular, William of Ecureuil, saved the mangonel from certain destruction, and it subsequently resumed its bombardment of the fortress. Raymon later surrendered the castle after a failed night-time escape attempt by the garrison.

▼ *This long exposure photograph shows a modern trebuchet launching a fireball. The trace of the fireball illustrates the trajectory of such weapons. (Martchan/Alamy)*

COUNTERWEIGHT TREBUCHETS

The exact place and time of origin of the counterweight trebuchet is, like much of the history of siege engines, hidden. What we can say with reasonable confidence, however, is that the first steps forwards were taken around the 11th and 12th centuries in the Middle East.

Some earlier tantalising sources refer to traction trebuchets with counterweight assistance to improve the rate of acceleration, and also allude to the possibility of pure counterweight trebuchets, but it is in the 1190s that the first clear statements of these weapons emerge, by which time they had also entered Western European history.

The basic configurations of the counterweight trebuchet are worth exploring a little before we go deeper into the

COUNTERWEIGHT TREBUCHET

The trebuchet here is of an advanced medieval type, with both a movable counterweight box, hinged to the end of the casting beam, plus a small additional fixed counterweight set at an angle above. Against the extreme weight at the front, the casting beam would be drawn into its launch position via the two windlasses on the rear of the frame, each linked to the casting arm with a pulley.

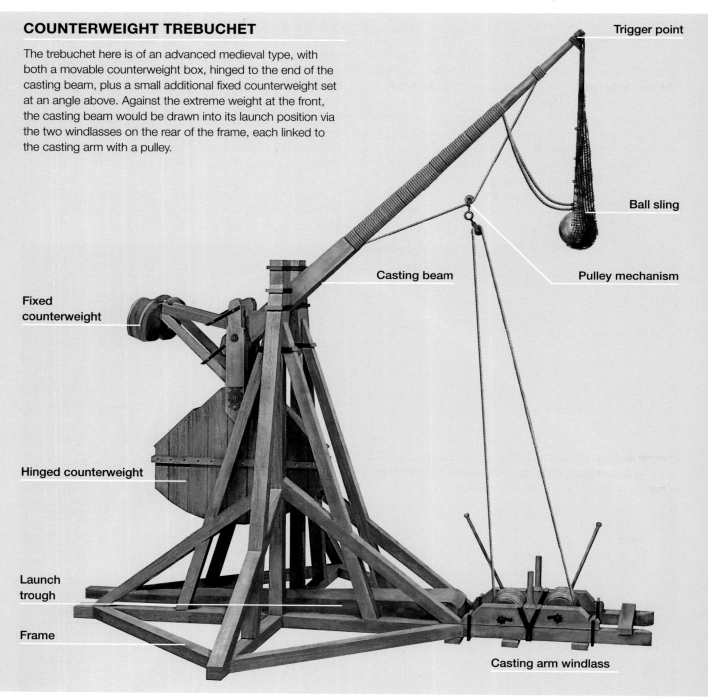

Trigger point

Ball sling

Casting beam

Pulley mechanism

Fixed counterweight

Hinged counterweight

Launch trough

Frame

Casting arm windlass

▶ *This very basic 15th-century depiction of a trebuchet illustrates how far forward the ball would sit in the launch trough towards the counterweight, prior to launch. (Konrad Kyeser/PD)*

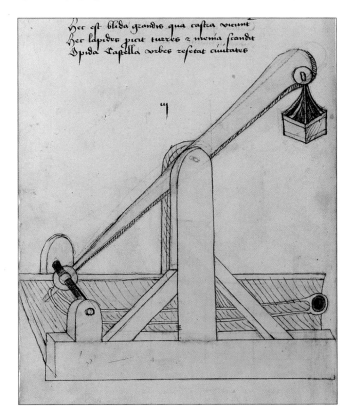

history. The key difference between the traction and counterweight trebuchets was, as the name implies, the replacement of manpower with a heavy weight to pull down the beam-sling arm on firing. The weights were at first typically sacks of rocks hung on the end of the beam, but later graduated to more sizeable (and heavier) items such as large crates containing wet sand, boulders and even blocks of iron or lead.

FIXED COUNTERWEIGHTS

Counterweights went through various evolutions during the history of trebuchets. The most basic type was the fixed counterweight, in which the weight was constructed as a rigid box onto, or integral with, the beam-sling arm. The fixed counterweight (what was known as a *trabicum* trebuchet) was simple to construct, but it did not provide the most efficient drop, as instead of sinking straight down to the ground (the quickest and most efficient route) it took an inward arc that was the opposite of the upward arcing path at the other end of the beam-sling.

A more sophisticated option, therefore, was a hinged counterweight (known as the *biffa*), in which the weight box was attached to the end of the short arm by means of a free-moving hinge. This arrangement meant that the counterweight remained pointing directly downward during its descent, and thus sank faster, providing better acceleration, enhanced leverage and therefore greater range potential. It was also easier to operate a trebuchet with a moveable counterweight; it was quicker to bring one of these to the ready position. The *tripantum* trebuchet had a movable counterweight that could

be adjusted upon the beam to alter the drop characteristics, and therefore the trajectory and velocity of the projectile. Note that the style of hinged counterweights would vary, the two most common options being a single box (looking rather like a traditional carpenter's toolbox) or two more slender symmetrical countweights set side-by-side.

Medieval military engineers in charge of trebuchets would have immersed themselves in a world of physical mathematics and experimentation. Historian of the medieval

▶ *This 15th-century image shows what appears to be a half-way stage between traction and counterweight trebuchet. (Timewatch Images/Alamy)*

▼ *Huge limestone trebuchet balls from Russia, shaped in the 15th–16th centuries. Stone masons were critical members of a trebuchet team. (PereslavlFoto/CC BY-SA 3.0)*

◄ *This medieval image of a counterweight trebuchet has suggestions of the 'squirrel wheel' cocking mechanism on the sides. (Chronicle/Alamy)*

siege, Jim Bradbury, has noted some the revelations of modern experimentation with trebuchets:

> A recent experiment with trebuchets was made in 1989 in Denmark, through the Museum of Falsters Minder. The researchers began with a series of models, and then constructed a full-scale trebuchet, with which a series of experimental throws was made, altering the variables, including the angle of the sling and the weight of the missile. They calculated that it required a twenty-seven ton counterweight to cast a 1,000 kg [2,205lb] stone. They found that the heavier the missile, the earlier the sling burst open. When operated, it went with a 'strange singing sound'. For example, a 15kg [33lb] concrete ball, operated by a one-ton counterweight, released at an angle of 70 degrees: 'accelerated away in a curved trajectory' to a distance of 120m [130yds]; the longest shot with a ball of this weight was 180m [200yds]. They claimed that their accuracy was as good as that of a modern mortar, and that the machine was both reliable and accurate.[6]

OPERATIONAL PROCEDURES

To operate the trebuchet, first the counterweight had to be raised and held in place. This feat required much mechanical assistance, given that counterweights could vary between 4 and 14 tonnes in weight. Given the huge weight, the job was usually performed through the use of winches or by the appropriately named 'squirrel wheels'. These were giant wooden wheels, not unlike the (far smaller, of course) hamster wheels found in household pet cages, with the wheel attached to the throwing beam by a winding rope. Members of the trebuchet team would literally climb inside the wheels and walk them around, taking about 5–6 minutes to hoist the counterweight into its elevated position, whereupon it was locked in place with a trigger mechanism. Note that the wheels then had to be 'unwound', slackening off the rope that had drawn the counterweight into position; if the counterweight were dropped with the wheels engaged, the resulting centrifugal forces would literally shatter the frame of the trebuchet.

The trebuchet's projectile was placed in the large pouch in the centre of the sling, ready for firing. Beneath the frame of the trebuchet was a long wooden trough that ran fully up to the front of the engine, beneath the counterweight. The stone, nestling in its pouch, was placed in the trough as far forwards as it could go, with the rest of the sling laid neatly in the trough with the tip of the throwing arm nearly resting upon the trough's rear end. This arrangement ensured that the stone

◄ *Walking inside the 'squirrel wheels' could be very disorientating, as light constantly flickered through the slats. (Martin Addison/CC BY-SA 2.0)*

▲ *The trebuchet at Warwick Castle, England, is one of the largest functional trebuchets in the world. It was built mainly following 13th-century plans. (Kumar Sriskandan/Alamy)*

▲ *The Warwick Castle trebuchet in action. Most of the mighty frame is made of oak, while the casting arm is of ash, which has greater flexibility. (Dennis Chang UK/Alamy)*

achieved maximum acceleration during launching, and also that the ball would travel in a true direction, directly lined up with the swing of the arm.

Upon firing, the trigger mechanism was initiated, the counterweight sank quickly downwards, and the throwing arm whipped upwards, dragging the sling and projectile back and upwards in a rapidly accelerating motion. The most popular mechanical method by which the sling actually released the ball at the top of its angle was the angle pin release, in which a loop at one end of the sling was slotted

loose over a fixed and angled pin in the top of the throwing arm. For much of the arm's travel, the loop was held in place by the forces of friction and tension, but at the top of the throw those forces were overcome and the loop slipped off the pin, allowing the pouch to open and the ball to travel onwards towards its target. The trebuchet shooter would be able to adjust the angle of the pin to control the point of release and therefore the point of impact. Once the trebuchet had been 'fired', reloading was a simply matter of repeating the process from the beginning.

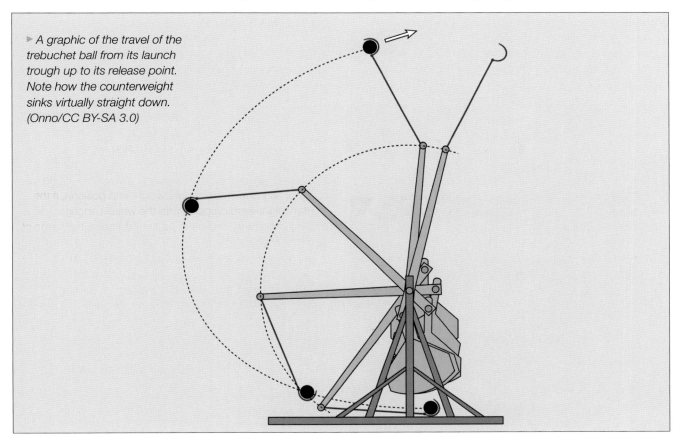

▶ *A graphic of the travel of the trebuchet ball from its launch trough up to its release point. Note how the counterweight sinks virtually straight down. (Onno/CC BY-SA 3.0)*

THE TREBUCHET AT WAR

Counterweight trebuchets were a feature of warfare right until the end of the Middle Ages. Even as cannon made their debut and then progressively established themselves as the artillery of choice, trebuchets continued in action for a good 150 years or so beyond the introduction of gunpowder weaponry.

There was a collection of reasons for the trebuchet's long-term success – better performance and greater reliability than the early cannon; lack of available cannon; scarcity of high-quality gunpowder; sheer habit. In fact, throughout the 14th and much of the 15th centuries we often see trebuchets serving alongside gunpowder artillery during sieges; the siege of Burgos (1475–6) and the siege of Rhodes (1480) are examples. One of the last recorded uses of the trebuchet was the siege of Tenochtitlán, now Mexico City but in 1521 the capital of the Aztec Empire. The city came under siege by the Spanish forces of Hernán Cortés, who had with them gunpowder artillery shipped all the way from Spain. When supplies of gunpowder ran low, Cortés ordered the construction of a large trebuchet to bombard the enemy defences. Unfortunately, the skill set required to construct and operate a trebuchet must also have been running short at this time, because the very first ball that was launched from the trebuchet simply went straight up, then came back down and obliterated the trebuchet. Comic value aside, this incident illustrates the point that, to be effective, trebuchets had to be operated by people who knew what they were doing.

RANGE AND ACCURACY

If they were operated by experts, then counterweight trebuchets were indeed capable of breaching walls, if those walls could be struck repeatedly and accurately. In capable hands, the accuracy of the trebuchet at maximum range was in the region of 5 × 5m (16½ft × 16½ft), sufficient to smash out a section of heavy wall over time. A notable illustration of this capability occurred during the siege of Acre in 1189–91, in which the Muslim forces of Saladin (r. 1174–93) resisted the siege of King Richard I (r. 1189–99).

In total the Crusaders had 11 trebuchets at their disposal, grouped in batteries to deliver heavy and regular bombardment. Following the standard practice of the time, the trebuchets were all given fearsome names, including 'God's Stone Thrower' and 'Bad Neighbour'. (Other examples from medieval history include 'Vicar', 'Throwing Bull', 'Lady' and 'Warwolf.) One of the best known chronicles of the Third Crusade, the *Itinerarium Peregrinorum et Gesta Regis Ricardi*, provides a brilliant insight into the use and application of counterweight trebuchets in its account of the siege, worth reproducing at length:

▼ *Trebuchets could throw all manner of objects at their enemies, including barrels of inflammable substances, as seen here. (PD)*

▲ *This trebuchet from a 15th-century manuscript shows a double-counterweight design, with each counterweight hinged on the casting beam. (Roberto Valturio/PD)*

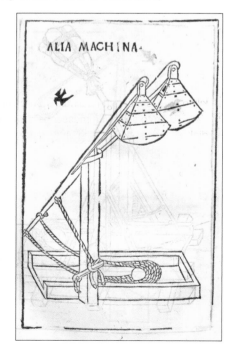

ALIA MACHINA·

▶ *A medieval impression of the siege of Antioch (1097–98) shows a traction trebuchet in action – note the way the pullers face towards the trebuchet. (PD)*

The king of France [Philip II, also a commander at the siege] made a swift recovery from his illness and concentrated on constructing siege engines and placing stonethrowers in suitable places. He arranged for these to fire continually day and night. He had one excellent one which he called 'Bad Neighbour' [*Malvoisine*]. The Turks in the city had another which they called 'Bad Relation' [*Mal Cousine*] which often used to smash 'Bad Neighbour' with its violent shots. The king kept rebuilding it until its continual bombardment partly destroyed the main city wall and shattered the Cursed Tower. On one side the duke of Burgundy's stonethrower had no little effect. On the other the Templars' trebuchet wreaked impressive devastation, while the Hospitallers' trebuchet also never ceased hurling, to the terror of the Turks.

Besides these, there was a trebuchet that had been constructed at general expense, which they called 'God's Stone-Thrower'. A priest, a man of great probity, always stood next to it preaching and collecting money for its continual repair and for hiring people to gather the stones for its ammunition. This machine at last demolished the wall next to the Cursed Tower for around two perches' length [10m/33ft].

The Count of Flanders had had a choice trebuchet, which King Richard had after his death, as well as another trebuchet which was not so good. These two constantly bombarded the tower next to a gate which the Turks frequently used, until the tower was half-demolished. Besides these, King Richard had two new ones made with remarkable workmanship and material which would hit the intended target no matter how far off it was. [...] He also had two mangonels prepared. One of these was so swift and violent that its shots reached the inner streets of the city meat market.

King Richard's stonethrowers hurled constantly by day and night. It can be firmly stated that one of them killed twelve men with a single stone. That stone was sent for Saladin to see, with messengers who said that the diabolical king of England had brought from Messina, a city he had captured, sea flint and the smoothest stones to punish the Saracens. Nothing could withstand their blows; everything was crushed or reduced to dust.[7]

▲ *A reenactor prepares to launch a trebuchet at Les Baux de Provence, France, with the ball positioned well forward in the launch trough. (Jon Davison/Alamy)*

CONSTRUCTION

Many important points about trebuchets in war emerge from this account. The first is that the trebuchets are constructed in situ at the site of the battle. In the days before truly efficient long-distance logistics, this was common in siege

▶ *This impression of a mangonel illustrates how multiple individuals could be assigned to each pulling rope, for maximum traction. (PD)*

warfare, although sometimes trebuchets were transported cross-country. Finding the materials for, and constructing, a trebuchet was an act of serious industry, involving many tonnes of timber and a large workforce. During the siege of Berwick, Scotland, in 1333, the Flemish merchant, pirate, soldier and siege engineer John Crabbe oversaw the production a two large trebuchets. A total of 40 oak trees were felled to supply the timber, after which a team of 24 oxen hauled the load to Cowik, Yorkshire, for construction. A huge team was assembled to make the weapons and their projectiles – just producing the stone balls required 37 stone masons and six quarrymen.

From the account of 'God's Stone Thrower', above, we can see how the trebuchets were indeed capable of taking down large sections of fortress walls – here a 10m (33ft) breach is opened up.

PSYCHOLOGICAL EFFECTS

This being said, like the mangonel, only part of the effect of the counterweight trebuchet was that of wall breaching. There was also the mental effect to consider – a prolonged

▲ This trebuchet at Dover Castle illustrates how trebuchets could also be used to hurl objects cleanly back over fortress walls, against besieging forces. (Robert Wyatt/Alamy)

SIEGE TACTICS: EFFECTS ON TARGET

We must be careful in concluding that the presence of a trebuchet meant a wall would surely fall. For a start, taking out a wall was a slow business; 'God's Stone Thrower' was only able to create such a large breach after several weeks of hammering away. For a very large trebuchet, the typical rate of fire was about two rounds an hour – which is why they were generally deployed in batteries, to up the rates of fire through sheer numbers. Nevertheless, there are many instances of sieges in which trebuchets were less than effective against their objectives. During two Portuguese sieges in 1387, several trebuchets hurled 10–12 major stones against the walls for a period of two weeks, but did almost no damage to the external walls, compensating a little by smashing in some roofs of internal buildings. It was noted, however, that 'the garrisons paid no attention to this, for their lodgings were well arched: and no engine or springald could hurt them with any stones they could throw'.[8] At the siege of Dunbar in 1336, the defenders mocked the apparent impotence of the attackers' trebuchets by using cloths to 'wipe off' the marks left by the deflected balls.

The problem for the operators of trebuchets was that, obviously, fortress walls were very thick, especially near the bottom, so anything but a very clean and direct strike would have partial effect. At longer ranges, the arcing trajectory of the trebuchet ball would often mean that it struck the masonry with a downward glancing blow, rather than the right-angle strike of direct-fire artillery, so the material attrition could be limited and gradual. Furthermore, even if a breach was achieved, it tended to be higher up the wall face, with the thicker lower sections remaining standing. Thus, even a breach often did not remove the need for escalade or bridging assault.

▲ This view of the trebuchet at Château de Castelnaud provides a good perspective on the length of the launch trough. (Château de Castelnaud/GNUFDL)

▲ *This replica trebuchet illustrates the disproportionate difference between the length of the casting beam in front of the fulcrum to that behind it. (Sanstein/CC BY 3.0)*

trebuchet bombardment would be particularly harrowing on the garrison and population of a fortress. Movement inside the fortress was fraught and tense, with eyes cast anxiously upwards at all times. Being indoors was no protection, as at any moment a giant stone ball might come smashing through a roof or tower wall. Entire upper sections of battlements might be swept away, carrying men, hoarding and merlons away with explosive force. Just the psychological and physical depredations of these huge incoming missiles could force a garrison to its knees. At the aforementioned siege of Berwick, for example, the besieging forces offered the town a respite from bombardment if they promised to surrender if they were not relieved by 20 July, 1333. The townspeople readily accepted these terms.

▼ *This basic outline of a trebuchet at Caerlaverock Castle gives an impression of the size of the counterweight, which would be filled with earth and stone. (Akinom/PD)*

DEFENSIVE USE

One final point to make about trebuchets, thinking back again to the siege of Acre, was that it was not only attackers who could make good use of these engines. Counterweight trebuchets were ideal for defensive counterfire, as their long throwing arm could hurl stones over the top of the battlements while the trebuchet team remained down behind the protective walls. In the siege of Acre we see what can be classed as a medieval artillery duel take place, with each side attempting to smash the other's trebuchets. These engagements must have been terrifying and panicky affairs; each shot provided target information, making it a race against time to strike first.

Trebuchets, therefore, could be a decisive element in the attacking or defensive outcome of a siege, and remain as the greatest motif of the age of siege warfare.

▼ *This 19th-century technical artwork demonstrates the arcs of movement of a counterweight trebuchet, plus provides a close-up of the pulley mechanism. (PD)*

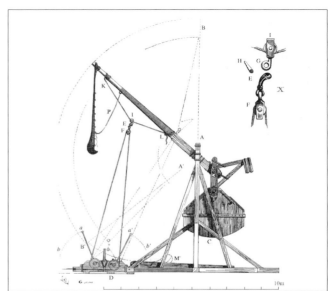

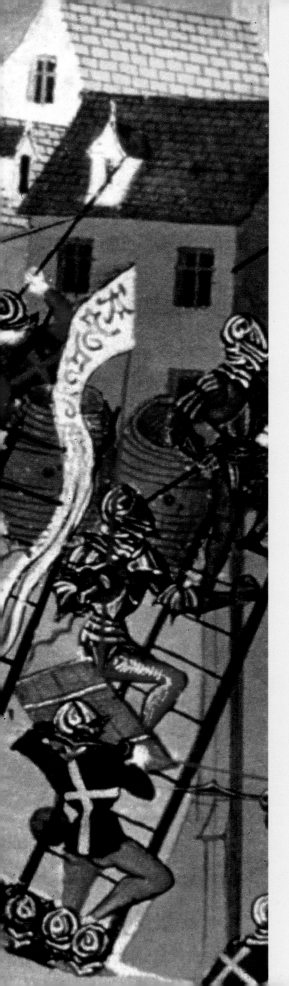

UNDER AND OVER: SIEGE TOWERS, UNDERMINING AND ESCALADE

If the walls of a fortress could not be breached by direct-impact weapons, then the besieging army had various other tactics and technologies at its disposal. These involved either assaulting up and over the walls or digging beneath them, and each option brought its own set of risks and advantages.

◄ *A relief from ancient Nineveh, Iraq, shows soldiers using ladders to scale walls in the 7th century* BC. *The assaulting troops are even firing bows as they climb. (Getty)*

MINING

While siege engines lent technological muscle to siege warfare, it was human muscle that largely decided the contest over a fortress. Nor was it just soldiers who were involved in the combat; during a siege a cast of other characters, including miners and sappers, brought their own unique set of skills in the effort to bring down the fortress walls and gain access to the interior.

Today we largely associate the word 'mine' with either a mineral extraction mine (e.g. a coal mine) or an explosive weapon emplaced underground and triggered by pressure or other force. If taken as a verb, the word also connotes the emplacement of these weapons. Yet if we scroll back into the ancient and medieval periods, all these meanings appear to coalesce in the practice of siege mining.

The overarching purpose of siege mining was straightforward enough: destabilize and bring down the opposing fortress walls by literally undermining their foundations. Mining could also be used to break through

▼ *Ogrodzieniec Castle in Poland is situated on top of the towering Castle Mountain. Its rocky and elevated terrain provided protection from undermining. (Shutterstock)*

into the interior of a fortress, providing a hidden route for a surprise assault by siege troops. Crucially, the key players in mining actions were, understandably, miners and sappers, not combat troops. As we shall see, however, their civilian origins and their underground activity by no means removed them from the risk of combat and violent death.

Undermining in siege warfare has ancient origins. One of the earliest visual references to the practice comes from a carved orthostat in the palace of Ashurnasirpal II (883–59 BC) at Nimrud, Assyria, dating back to the 9th century BC; in the detail, we can see a miner digging his way under the foundations of a city under siege. Historical references to undermining increase in frequency as we pass through antiquity, and the tactics of sapping and mining emerge in a codified form in Aeneas Tacticus, Vitruvius and Vegetius,

▲ A medieval manuscript shows, in crude fashion, sappers undermining a castle. The man underground, on the right, is carrying out the spoil from the digging. (PD)

▶ Effective escalade required that the besieging army maintained a constant flow of troops to the top of the escalade ladders. (PD)

amongst others. In one sense, undermining is one of the most enduring tactics in the history of warfare; it was still being practised, albeit with the purpose of emplacing huge quantities of underground explosives, in World War I.

ADVANTAGES

So why was undermining used? Thinking first about the besieging forces, undermining had some advantages of economy and risk reduction. Large siege engines and direct overland assaults tended to be costly in both financial and human terms, whereas a mining operation could be conducted with a relatively small body of efficient mine workers plus the requisite timber to shore up the tunnels created. (Major mining actions could, of course, require a very large host of workers.) If done properly, furthermore, mining operations had a high likelihood of success, able to bring down walls that would otherwise require prolonged hails of boulders from the largest siege engines. For example, in 1216, Dover Castle on the south-east coast of England was besieged by Prince Louis of France. The castle was pummelled by catapults, trebuchets and a battering ram, but it was a mine that in the end brought down one of the gatehouse towers.

Undermining also offered the advantages of secrecy. Siege engines and direct assaults were conspicuous events, and observant defenders would often see the subtle – or overt – signs of their preparation even before their deployment. Undermining, by contrast, could take place day and night without the awareness of the enemy. The entrance to the gallery might be a significant distance from the fortress, or naturally concealed by woodland, which made it almost undetectable to the fortress garrison, and also made the job of disposing of the spoil somewhat easier.

LIMITATIONS AND DISADVANTAGES

So far, so good for undermining. Yet in many ways it was not the tactic of choice for besieging forces. It was, in fact something of a last resort, despite the advantages.

Time

For a start, undermining could take considerable time. The duration depended upon factors such as the distance from the mine entrance to the fortification and the nature of the terrain through which the gallery or sap would be

▼ This medieval engraving shows how undermining could also be used by the defenders, who have created a fire chamber beneath a siege tower. (PD)

▲ *Civilian miners, such as those in this 17th-century German illustration, were often used to deliver undermining operations. Attempts to use regular soldiers usually ended in unnecessary fatalities. (Deutsche Fotothek/PD)*

cut. Particularly in the medieval period, by which time castle builders were acutely sensitive to the threat of undermining, castles were often sited on high plateaus of solid rock – in Britain, think of national landmarks such as Edinburgh Castle – and/or with the extensive water defences surrounding the outer curtain wall, such as Caerphilly Castle. Both of these landscape defences could make undermining virtually impossible for all but the most stubborn siege commanders.

Even in suitable ground, digging a mine could take weeks, if not months, to perform, depending on the terrain. Nor was the timing predictable. Tunnel collapses, sudden military developments above ground and changes in the seasons could all render a tunnel network either redundant or delayed. But some hardy siege commanders were not dismayed by time or adversity. Undermining operations against St Andrews Castle in Fife, Scotland, in 1546–47, by the Earl of Arran went on for no less than 14 months, partly because the miners were digging into a foundation of solid rock (showing that a rock foundation did not make undermining entirely impossible). In places the mine shafts

UNDERMINING AND COUNTERMINING OPERATIONS

Here we have a graphical representation of mining and countermining operations. The besieging army (blue arrow) has dug a mine out from its positions, opening up into a fire chamber beneath one of the corner towers.

The defenders, meanwhile, have dug their own tunnel out from the fortress, intercepting the enemy tunnel at the fire chamber. The defenders then light a sulphorous fire, using bellows to blow the smoke down into the enemy tunnel structure.

1 Entrance to undermining tunnel
2 Entrance to defensive tunnel
3 Attackers' fire chamber
4 Defenders' tunnel
5 Defenders' fire to smoke out attackers
6 Castle tower (objective of undermining operation)

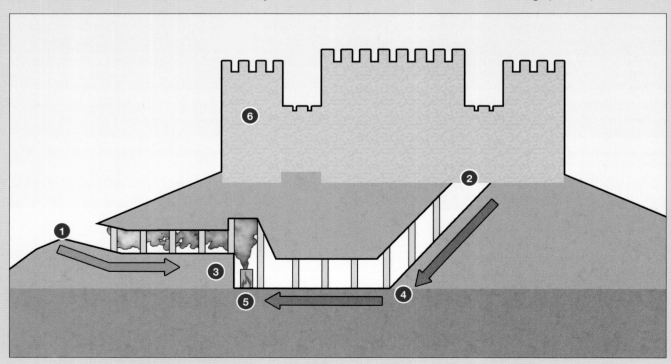

► *An undermining operation begins under the cover of an artillery barrage, mid 16th century. Note the multiple tunnel entrances, denoting different objectives. (Chronicle/Alamy)*

and galleries measured 1.8m (6ft) wide and 2.1m (7ft) high, dimensions that were very generous in absolute terms and particularly regarding the material through which they were digging. We do have evidence that, under the right conditions, a mine could be dug with gusty pace. Polybius recounts the tale that a group of miners, working in rotation throughout day and night, managed to produce 65m (70yds) of tunnel in just three days.

Man power

Another limitation on undermining actions was the problem of sourcing personnel. Mining was, and remains, a highly skilled manual occupation, with proper understanding of the geological challenge and all the myriad technicalities of digging out a tunnel that did not promptly collapse back on its occupants. During our periods of history, specialist engineering personnel were a rarity in the ranks of armies. For undermining operations, therefore, a besieging army had to draw civilian mineral miners into military service, either willingly (relatively speaking) from its home populations or by dragging unwilling but suitably skilled slaves, prisoners or local people into the operation. In many cases, and particularly in those regions without a mining industry, it might prove impossible to find the right number of people with the right abilities. On other occasions, however, sheer force of will and a general disdain for the lives of unskilled labour meant that a siege commander might have a large cast of people at his disposal. During the siege of Rhodes in 1522, for example, the Ottoman sultan Suleiman (r. 1520–66) included in his army of 200,000 men possibly around 2,000–3,000 mine workers. It was this sheer volume of personnel that enabled Suleiman to overcome the ingenious and industrious countermeasures of the defending Knights Hospitallers, eventually digging more tunnels than the fortress occupants could counter.

So, undermining was a problematic business at the best of times. Yet it remained a core part of siege warfare tactics throughout and beyond our period. Sometimes it was applied on account of sheer lack of choice. During the great siege of King's Castle, Limerick, Ireland in 1642, the besieging Irish Catholic Confederate general Garrett Barry had no siege artillery to speak of, and undermining remained his best option for bringing down the defenders' walls. Often, undermining was part of a blended strategy, however, with intensive warfare raging above the ground while the siege commander conducted undermining to hedge his bets.

TOOLS AND PREPARATION

The actual techniques of digging a siege mine are basic in description, but bely much devil in the detail. Essential mining tools were picks, shovels, mattocks, chisels and hammers to hack away the rock, and baskets, hand barrows and wheelbarrows to carry away the spoil. Miners had the expertise to be able to 'read' the ground around them, knowing how to make the most efficient cuts with their tools, and what contours and masses to avoid cutting to maintain roof integrity. Mine-related carpentry was also a very specialized skill. The carpenters were responsible for making the load-bearing frames that were installed as the mine progressed in length. Some of the most detailed analysis of the construction of these frames comes from siege historian Kenneth Wiggins, from his very detailed study of the siege of Limerick. A section of his analysis is worth quoting:

The quality of the excavated evidence at Limerick is such that we can form an accurate picture of how the mines and countermines were constructed. When a gallery was to be opened at the bottom of an entrance shaft, the first rectangular timber frame was established. A frame was

▲ *King John's Castle in Limerick, Ireland, was attacked in 1641 with undermining operations, which eventually forced the castle's surrender. (William Murphy/CC BY-SA 2.0)*

▼ *This 17th-century illustration shows different approaches taken by undermining operations, to negotiate terrain and defences. (BL 534i7, British Library)*

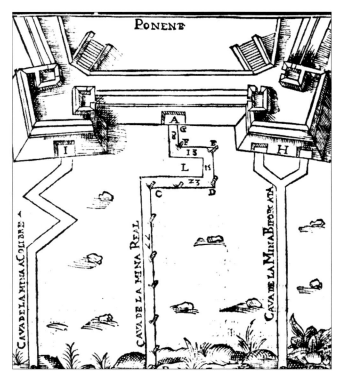

made of four members: a baseplate, mortised at both ends, which was laid transversely across the floor of the mine; two vertical props for the sides, each with a foot tenon that was inserted into a baseplate mortise; a horizontal top-plate completed the frame by connecting the opposed pair of props and was secured by mortise-and-tenon joinery. The frames were installed along the length of a gallery at intervals of between 32cm and 76cm. The sectional dimensions of the galleries, controlled by the size of the timber frames, varied between 1.16 metres and 1.61 metres in width and by between 1.4 metres and 1.6 metres in height. To prevent subsistence, the overhead gaps between the frames were filled with slotted-in timber planks, supported by the top-plates, and the side gaps were often covered with pointed timber strips, inserted between adjacent pairs of props.[1]

The construction of these frames naturally had to be done to rigorous standards. The pressures from above could be simply enormous, especially in the tunnel sections that ran under the fortress walls itself.

This description might give the impression of a considered and careful engineering project. The demands of the siege, however, meant that there was always the pressure to cut corners in an already dangerous undertaking. The lives of miners were threatened constantly by tunnel collapses or the build-up of dangerous gases underground – during the siege of Lincoln in 1143, no fewer than 80 miners and workers died of suffocation. Sheer exhaustion and physical injury would also lay low many of the workers.

SIEGE TACTICS: UNDERMINING OBJECTIVES AND LAYOUTS

Despite the dangers of the undermining work, the objective remained focused. To precipitate wall collapse, the tunnel had to be worked under a major section of wall or a tower, keep or other critical structure. Once the tunnel had reached the wall, directly under its foundations, it was typically widened out into a larger chamber, supported by props and timber. When the chamber had reached sufficient dimensions (at least the depth of the wall above and many metres across), if was filled with brushwood, firewood, resinous timber and flammable fats; during the siege of Rochester in 1215, the fat of some 40 pigs was applied to the materials to encourage vigorous burning. The flammable materials were then put to the torch, with the resulting fire eventually burning through the support props, leading to the collapse of the chamber and, all going to plan, the wall or tower above it. With the later invention of gunpowder, a more rapid option for the collapse of the chamber was to stack barrels of powder around the struts, light the fuse, and beat a hasty retreat. To contain the force of the explosion, however, the chamber entrance was filled in with bricks and earth. Historical evidence for the use of explosive mines begins to emerge around the end of the 15th century, in Spain and Italy.

Siege mines varied extensively in their complexity, length, number of galleries and configurations. Some were little more than a solitary tunnel and chamber, targeted at a single identifiable part of the defences. Others consisted of multiple tunnels branching out in complex patterns beneath the fortress and surrounding area. Siege mines still survive today underneath Bungay Castle in Suffolk, which was besieged in 1174 by royalist forces, when the lord of the castle, the Earl

▲ *Siege mining had to be concealed as much as possible from the enemy. Wicker barricades and screens might be used to screen the tunnel entrance. (Michiel Colijn/PD)*

of Norfolk, joined the rebellion against Henry II. Undermining played a key role in the fortress's eventual subjugation, and archaeological investigations in the 1930s exposed one of the mines, which terminates under the castle in a distinctive cruciform pattern, formed by two lateral galleries.

▼ *Bungay Castle in Bungay, Suffolk, was another medieval castle defeated by undermining operations, during a short siege in 1194. (Scott Anderson/CC BY 2.0)*

SAPPING

Digging out the foundations of a fortress wall or tower did not necessarily involve going underground. Another option was to stay above the ground, and order men to work at the base of the wall or tower, hacking out masonry or digging directly down underneath the foundations. As the sappers destabilised the fortress, they supported the wall with timber props until the moment came, as with undermining, when the whole structure was set on fire.

Naturally, the big issue for such overground operations was protecting the sappers and labourers from the inevitable shower of missiles targeting them from the battlements. There were essentially three ways of doing this.

DIGGING TORTOISE

In deep antiquity, especially in the case of the Assyrians, the sappers would simply advance under the cover of large shields, featuring pronounced curves to help deflect the boulders and other weights dropped from above. Another option was to dig a trench out from the siege lines to the

▼ *A reconstruction drawing of mining under the North Gate East tower of Dover Castle, during the siege there in 1216. (Heritage Image Partnership Ltd/Alamy)*

fortress defences, and at the same time erect a wood and earth shelter framework above it to protect the occupants.

The most advanced option, however, was to move the men up to the wall under the cover of a digging tortoise. This was essentially the tortoise device already described in previous chapters, but minus armaments such as rams. (In other, lighter versions, the tortoise was unwheeled, and the protective shed was literally lifted and carried by its occupants and deposited where required. In Roman terminology this shelter was known as a *vinea* or *ampela*.) A key difference of the digging tortoise from other offensive tortoise designs was that, according to some ancient descriptions, it had a flat face that could sit flush up against the enemy wall, enabling the men inside to work right up against their objective. A triangular roof profile deflected the missiles thumping down from above.

Ditch-filling tortoise

One interesting variant of the tortoise that should be mentioned is the ditch-filling tortoise, attested to in Greek and Roman sources, such as accounts by Philo Mechanicus, Athenaeus and Vitruvius.

In contrast to the digging tortoise, the ditch-filling tortoise was intended to provide men with a protected environment in which to fill-in ditches and other terrain obstacles, in preparation for siege towers and other wheeled vehicles moving forwards up to the fortress walls. Siege towers especially were vulnerable to tipping over if the ground was uneven or pitted, and if they were filled with fighting men, lives as well as machinery would be lost. According to descriptions from Athenaeus, the ditch-filling tortoise was entirely enclosed, with the base of the frame about 10m (33ft) square. All sides inclined inwards, rather like a four-sided pyramid, meeting at the top in a transverse ridge. In Athaneaus' model, furthermore, the four wheels of the device, one at each corner of the undercarriage (*escharion*) were directionally adjustable, to enable the whole mighty contraption to move sideways as well as forwards and backwards

▶ *A flared talus, at the base of a castle wall or tower, spread the ground pressure of the structure, and therefore made it less vulnerable to undermining. (Shutterstock)*

SAPPING UNDER COVER

Sapping towards a castle exposed the soldiers to all manner of defensive fire from the battlements, hence protective shelters were typically built overhead. These shelters were largely built in the same manner as wood-framed tortoises, hide-covered to guard against fire. Here we see a shelter deployed across a moat, to enable the men to cross the water safely (or deploy ditch-filling technologies) and then sap under a fortress tower.

1 Wood-framed shelter (protected with hides) for sappers
2 Sheltered passageway for sappers
3 Wooden supports embedded in the moat bank.
4 Moat/wet ditch
5 Sapping/undermining works
6 Castle tower foundations

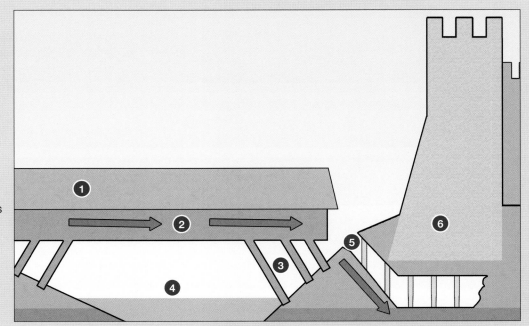

COUNTERMEASURES AGAINST SAPPING AND MINING

Fortress commanders were perfectly aware of the perils presented by undermining and sapping, and were ever inventive in thinking up ways to find out whether this kind of activity was happening, and devising countermeasures against it.

DETECTION

Defeating undermining naturally began with detecting the mining activity in the first place. This was not easy by sheer observation alone, as the opponents would be doing their best to control the entrance and the disposal of spoil. One tactic, for example, would be to conceal the entrance to the tunnel under the framework of a siege tower, following the principle of 'hiding in plain sight'. In other instances, simple wooden or wattle screens were erected to hide the breaking of ground.

Technology and some basic science came to the aid of the besieged. All underground excavations create minor seismic effects, and the vibrations emanating from the digging could be detected. Simple measures included standing bowls of water on the ground and observing them

▼ *Wheeled shelters provided useful shields under which sappers could work. The illustration comes from Hans Talhoffer (1420–90). (Det Kongelige Bibliotek/PD)*

for vibration-induced ripples running across the surface of the water. Delicate and finely balanced bells might also be set on slender poles inserted into the ground; the vibrations from the ground would transmit up the pole and set the bells tinkling. Similarly, we hear of thin bronze shields or resonant copper vessels being set into the earth, and giving out a delicate chiming noise in response to mining activity. Polybius' *Histories* provides an insight into such detection technologies, and also the response to undermining once it was detected, in the case of the Aetolian resistance during the Aetolian War of 191–189 BC. In one siege action:

> The Aetolians [...] offered a gallant resistance to the assault of the siege artillery and [the Romans], therefore, in despair had recourse to mines and underground tunnels. Having safely secured the central one of their three works, and carefully concealed the shaft with wattle screens, they erected in front of it a covered walk or stoa about two hundred feet long, parallel with the wall; and beginning digging from that, they carried it on unceasingly day and night, working in relays. For a considerable number of days, the besieged did not discover them carrying the earth away through the shaft; but when the heap of earth thus brought out became too high to be concealed from those inside the city, the commanders of the besieged garrison set to work vigorously digging a trench inside, parallel to the wall and to the stoa which faced the towers. When the trench was made to the required depth, they next placed in a row along the side of the trench nearest the wall a number of brazen vessels made very thin; and, as they walked along the bottom of the trench past these, they listened for the noise of the digging outside. Having marked the spot indicated by any of these brazen vessels, which were extraordinarily sensitive and vibrated to the sound outside, they began digging from within, at right angles to the trench, another underground tunnel leading under the wall, so calculated as to exactly hit the enemy's tunnel. This was soon accomplished, for the Romans had not only brought their mine up to the wall, but had under-pinned a considerable length of it on either side of their mine; and thus the two parties found themselves face to face.[2]

COUNTERMINING

This account illustrates how the bronze vessels could not only identify the fact that digging was underway, but with a bit of intelligent interpretation (probably involving a measure of triangulation between vessels) the general direction and

▶ *The Roman* testudo *formations involved packed infantry, with their shields locked together tightly enough, acording to this illustration, for ladderless escalade. (Justus Lipsius/PD)*

depth of a tunnel could be detected. Here the defenders opt for countermining as a response, literally attempting the underground interception of the enemy miners. Countermining brought all the attendant risks and efforts of undermining, and was very much dependent on the besieged having the right personnel and resources within their walls. Props and frames, for example, might have been made by stripping down buildings of their woodwork.

Once mine met countermine, especially if unexpectedly, then brutal underground fighting could ensue. The close-quarters violence was often fought with the tools of the mining trade, lit dim and red by fluttering oil lamps in a scene of Hadean horror.

Smoke

For the countermining operation a better option was to try to fill the enemy tunnel with smoke, usually created by setting fire to brushwood or similar materials, punching a hole or multiple holes through into the enemy gallery, then blowing the smoke through the holes by means of bellows. Such ingenuity was seen during the Roman siege of Ambracia in 189 BC. The Ambracians, having detected a Roman mine, tunnelled down until they found the enemy mine shaft. Into the shaft they inserted a large clay jar filled with chicken feathers, capping the jar with an iron lid full of holes. They then filled the space around the jar with earth, leaving two gaps, one either side, for holes through which spears could be jabbed, to keep the attackers away from the jar. 'They then took a pair of bellows such as blacksmiths use, and, having attached them to the orifice of the funnel, they vigorously blew up the fire placed on the feathers near the mouth of the jar, continually withdrawing the funnel in proportion as the feathers became ignited lower down. The plan was successfully executed; the volume of smoke created was very great, and, from the peculiar nature of feathers, exceedingly pungent, and was all carried into the faces of the enemy. The Romans, therefore, found themselves in a very distressing and embarrassing position, as they could neither stop nor endure the smoke in the mines.'[3] The burning feathers would have also released a poisonous sulphur compound, thus making this action an early example of chemical warfare.

An example of sulphur more directly applied in siege warfare comes from the siege of Dura-Europos (in Syria) in 256 AD, where the Romans this time were the defenders, trying to keep out the Sassanian Persians. The Persians had launched undermining operations against the fortress, and the Romans responded with a countermine that eventually broke through into one of the Persian galleries. The Persians, however, had heard the Romans coming, and lit a fire upon which they threw

sulphur and bitumen. Again using bellows to drive the smoke into the Roman tunnel, they killed 19 Romans through sulphur dioxide poisoning, as revealed in subsequent archaeological investigations. The same investigations have also uncovered the skeleton of one Persian in the tunnel, probably an individual overcome by the gases he himself had created.

▶ *A 15th-centruy artwork suggests the horrors of escalade, a defending soldier preparing to smash the climber with a rock as he surmounts the wall. (Classic Image/Alamy)*

Fire

Another description of a countermining action, towards the end of the medieval period, comes from the Venetian physician Nicolo Barbaro, eyewitness to the siege of Constantinople in 1453 by the Turks. The following account is also insightful for explaining how men with relevant skills were found from the city's population:

> On this day, the sixteenth of May, there took place on land the following events. The Turks had dug a mine, to get into the city under the walls, and the mine was discovered on this day. The Turks had begun to dig it half a mile from the city walls, and it passed under the foundations; but our men in the city heard them working at night, with the digging of this mine, which had already passed under the foundations of the walls. As soon as this noise was heard, the Megaduke at once informed the Most Serene Emperor of it, and he was told of the stage which the mine had reached. The Emperor wondered greatly at this, and quickly arranged for action to be taken about the mine. At once a search was made throughout the city for all the men experienced in mining, and when they were found, they were sent for by the Megaduke, who had them dig a mine inside the city, to find the Turkish one, and one tunnel met the other in such a way that ours found theirs, and our men were prepared for this, and quickly threw fire into theirs and burned all the props supporting it, so that the earth collapsed on top of the Turks and suffocated those who were in the mine or they were burned in the fire. This mine was at a place called Calegaria, and the Turks put it there because there were no barbicans. It caused great fear in the city, because it was thought that the Turks might make an attack any night by way of their mines, although on this occasion they were discomfited. Nothing else happened on this day, except for a great deal of cannon fire in the usual way, and such shouting that the very air seemed to be splitting apart.[4]

Other accounts of the delights inserted into siege tunnels were bee hives, wasp nests, angry (or in reality, terrified) big cats and even wild bears.

Missiles

The procedures for defending against sapping attacks above ground largely involved dropped missiles. If a digging tortoise or similar shelter was at the base of a wall, the defenders atop that wall would drop the full spectrum of heavy objects and harmful liquids down on top of the tortoise. Another option was to send out a sortie from one of postern gates, and attack the diggers – because the sappers were often civilian miners or labourers rather than professional military personnel, experienced soldiers could typically overcome them quickly in open combat.

▶ *A 15th-century illustration showing mathematical considerations of undermining, from Gabriello Busca's* Della Espugnatione *(1585). (BL 62.b.15; British Library)*

AENEAS TACTICUS ON MINE DETECTION AND COUNTERMINES

'If you think you are being undermined, the trench outside must be dug to a great depth, so that the enemy's mine will open into the trench and their men will be seen plainly at work. Where you have enough material, you should also build a wall in the trench, using the strongest and largest stones you can get. If you have no stones to build a wall, bring all pieces of wood you can find, and if the mine runs up against the trench at any point, there pile up logs and the odd pieces of wood, and set light to them, covering up all other faces of the pile, so that the smoke passes into the enemy's workings, and stifles the men at work there; it is even possible that many of them will die in suffocation. ... If, however, you know at what spot they are digging, you should dig countermines and engage them underground, barring their progress and burning them out. There is an old story in this connexion, Amasis, while besieging Barca, started to dig mines. The citizens, on realizing his intention, were greatly dismayed, fearing that he would defeat their vigilance, until a smith thought out a plan, which was to go round inside the walls with a bronze part of a shield and apply it to the ground. There was no sound where the shield was applied, except at the point where the mines were being dug. There the mining caused it to ring. Here then the men of Barca dug countermines and killed many of the enemy's miners. So this method is still employed at night in discovering the whereabouts of mines. I have now described the best method of defence. ... When you are starting mining operations yourself, the following will prove the most effective screen. Take two carts, and tilt them up together from behind like opening doors, until their poles are high in the air and converge towards the same point; and tie the poles together. Next on this framework bind other poles and wickerwork, or anything else to serve as a screen above, and daub the whole with clay. The wheels will enable you to bring [it] ... wherever you want it, and to take it away afterwards, and under this shelter the miners can work.'[3]

OVER THE TOP

Undermining and sapping were important techniques in the siege commander's tactical toolbox. Yet a larger number of sieges were ultimately settled by soldiers going over the walls, not under them. One only need to make a cursory glance at a medieval castle or ancient fortress to realize what a challenge this could be.

Fortress walls towered tens of metres over the battlefield, and were designed specifically to stop people surmounting them. The tops would typically be crowded with defenders, each of them fighting with the tenacity of sheer survival to prevent any enemy soldier putting a foot on the battlements. Moreover, there remains today the classic tactical reality that it is harder to attack an objective above you than one that is below you; never is that reality more applicable than in siege warfare. But performed with intelligence, coordination and the application of relevant siege engines, a disciplined army could still ascend even the mightiest walls.

EMBANKMENTS

During ancient history, one popular method for assaulting the top of a wall, or at least getting close to it, was the use of an embankment, known as an *agger* in Latin or *chromata* in Greek. This was literally a long slope that began somewhere around the siege lines and finished at a point high up the fortress walls. The purpose of the embankment was either to deploy assaulting troops straight up it and over the walls, or to use the slope to send rams, siege towers and other

▲ *A depiction of the Arab conquest of Syracuse (878* AD*) illustrates how escalade manoeuvres were performed with both shields and swords. (Madrid Skylitzes/PD)*

▼ *An engraving from* Poliorceticon sive de machinis tormentis telis *(1605) by Justus Lipsius shows a Roman siege tower set on a man-made embankment. (World History Archive/Alamy)*

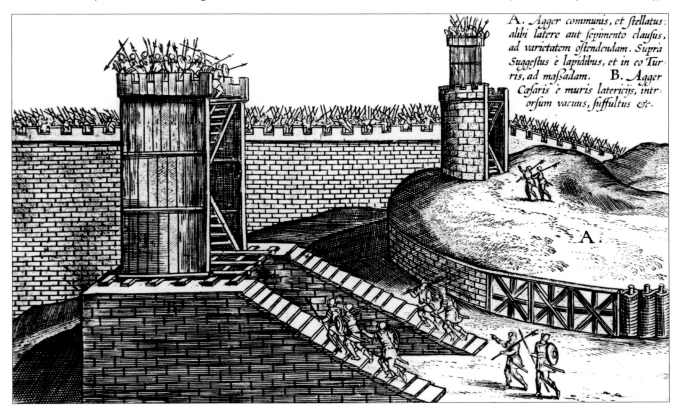

engines against the upper parts of the walls, which were typically thinner than the lower parts.

The tactical use of embankments appears as early as the 3rd millennium BC, and was particularly popular amongst Assyrian, Persian and Roman forces, mainly because they could draw into action the thousands of labourers and slave workers that were needed to produce one of these industrious feats. And feats they were. As Konstantin Nossov explains:

> Even in ancient Babylon they knew how to calculate the amount of the earth needed for the construction of an embankment, proceeding from the height of the wall. The distance from the wall to the place where the construction was to begin was always believed to be 60 metres [200ft] (a distance slightly exceeding the effectiveness of the range of bows and arrows at that time). Knowing the amount of earth needed, it is not difficult to calculate the number of workers and the amount of time required. One labourer working 12 hours a day could dig out and carry about two cubic metres of earth a day. Consequently, it would take 9,500 men working for five days to build an embankment reaching the top of a 22-meter-high [72ft 2in] wall. Of course, this calculation is for idealized conditions. Things that could potentially slow the work process, like filling up the moat, or incessant fire conducted by the besieged, have not been taken into account. These impediments would certainly increase the time required for the operation. but the main conclusion is that, given the necessary amount of labour, the construction of an embankment could be carried out at relatively short notice.[5]

Nossov's calculations of the numbers of men required for creating an embankment are an indication of why such tactics were rarely if ever used in the medieval period. Embankments were for times when empires had huge banks of expendable manpower, which the more limited states of medieval Europe rarely possessed.

Construction

Whatever the dimensions or distance of an embankment, building one was always going to be a manpower hungry and time-consuming process. There were some rudimentary methods of hastening the construction. The composition of the slope, for example, did not need be of plain earth cut straight out of the ground. Any volume-bulking materials could be used, including trees and the masonry from dismantled enemy outer buildings. If the embankment was purely intended for human beings to scramble up to the top of the walls, then the slope could be at steeper angles and therefore of shorter distance. If, however, the embankment was required for the deployment of siege engines, it had to have a smooth upper surface, a solid composition (to take the weight of the engine) and a gradual slope of about 30 degrees. The Hellenistic Greeks and the Romans developed a systematic method of constructing such embankments, forming the slope's gradient from layers of logs packed with earth, with the upper surface smoothed – if there was time – through hard-packed small stones bonded together with mortar. Of course, the labours of the workers were complicated by the constant barrage of arrows and other missiles fired down upon them. To enable work to proceed, therefore, the workers operated behind large shields or similar barricades embedded into the earthwork in front of them. In return, they relied on covering fire from their own side to suppress the enemy on the battlements.

Defensive countermeasures

The attempt to establish the siege embankment could result in a strange battle of industry between the two sides. One countermeasure against the embankment was for the fortress garrison to dig a mine out under their own walls and under the embankment itself, using the tunnel then to undermine the embankment. A notable example of this action was seen at the Persian siege of Palaepaphos in 498 BC.

Here the defenders of the Cypriot town used five tunnels to undercut the huge embankment that the Persians had constructed up to their battlements, with the defensive tunnels going down to depths of about 2.4m (8ft) and in some instances extending to distances of 20m (65ft) from their start point. The embankment was a materially complicated affair: historian Duncan Campbell notes that 'In addition to earth, field stones, and tree trunks, there were more than 1,000 architectural and sculptural fragments; these pieces, which include statues, sphinxes, lions and altars, are thought

◄ *Boarding bridges offered the advantage of being able to put a mass of soldiers onto the enemy battlements simultaneously, to overwhem defenders. (PD)*

to have come from a religious precinct, demolished by the Persians.'[6] From archaeological evidence, it appears that the defenders' plan was to create fire chambers under the each tunnel, collapsing these to cause the subsidence of the slope. An alternative to them would have been literally to extract the embankment material and carry it back inside their fortress, such as was attempted at the siege of Plataea in 429 BC,[7] but the hefty and awkward nature of the materials used in the embankment probably prevented this. The attempts to defeat the embankment failed, and the Persians eventually flooded over the walls and took the town.

Another great embankment siege was that put in place by the Romans against the Jewish town of Yodfat, or Jotapata, in 67 AD during the First Jewish–Roman War (66–73 AD). During this epic 47-day siege, the Romans constructed a siege ramp, but in response the defenders simply raised the height of their own walls. This led to a 'race to the top' which eventually the Romans won; the Roman soldiers surmounted the walls, passed into the city, and butchered thousands of people within.

ESCALADE

Theoretically, the simplest and one of the very oldest tactics for putting men over the walls of a fortress was escalade – climbing up and over the defences using ladders. Modern

▲ *A reconstruction drawing of a French siege tower and earth works at the siege of Dover Castle, 1216. Note the protective hides and the open access at the rear. (Heritage/Alamy)*

▼ *A Japanese iron* kaginawa *climbing hook. Grappling hooks could be used to ascend fairly low and relatively uncontested sections of wall. (Samuraiantiqueworld/CC-BY-SA-3.0)*

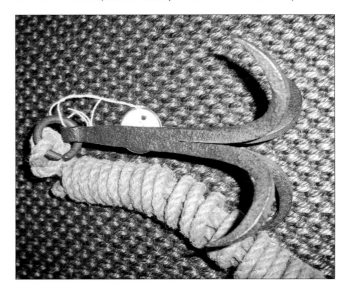

▲ *Escalade was a critical tactic used in the Byzantine capture of Antioch in 969* AD. *The figure at the top is the Byzantine general Michael Bourtzes. (PD)*

◄ *A rather decorous image of escalade taking place at the siege of Antioch in 1097–98. It was better to have the top of the ladder hook onto the battlements. (PD)*

special forces still train in escalade for use in hostage-rescue and building-assault operations, and, as they will tell you, escalade's apparent simplicity belies a testing reality.

The ladders

The primary tool of escalade was the scaling ladder. There were several varieties, including rope ladders, hemp ladders and what were essentially large scaling nets. Yet the most common variety were fixed-length wooden ladders, sometimes with iron hooks fitted at the top to hook more securely onto the parapet, while spikes at the bottom of the legs dug into the ground. In some instances, we see evidence of wheeled siege ladders, to enable them to be pushed along a wall rather like a traditional library ladder. Folding ladders were also used, and Apollodorus of Damascus, a Syrian-Greek engineer writing in the 2nd century AD, also explains how variable-length scaling ladders could be assembled from 3.5m (11ft 6in) interconnecting ladder sections, the ladders fastened together with wooden and iron bolts. Whatever the case, the ladders had to be extremely robust, as during action they would have to carry several soldiers at any one time, all of them burdened with weapons and possibly wearing armour. Get it wrong and the results could be disastrous – during the nine-month siege of Antioch in 1097–98 by the Crusading knights, ladders actually broke during an escalade attack, killing or injuring men from the fall.

Although it is unclear whether such multi-section ladders were actually used in combat, they did address the central problems of escalade – creating ladders that were the right length for the walls they would be used to assault. Typically, the scaling ladders would be bespoke to the context of a specific fortress. Estimating the height of the ladder was actually not as easy as it sounded, particularly if the siege lines were initially some distance away from the fortress. An

error in length of just a couple of metres could mean that the climbing soldier was unable to make the final step over the battlements, or that the angle of the ladder against the wall was either too steep or too shallow – the former made the climber and the ladder more exposed to enemy missiles and to slippage against a wall, while the latter meant it was easier for the ladder to be pushed away or to topple under the bouncing energies of multiple climbing men. Thus, correctly estimating the height of a wall was critical, and Vegetius explained how it should be done:

> Scaling ladders and other machines are of great use in mounting the walls, but cannot fulfil that purpose unless they exceed the height of the ramparts of the place. There are two methods of taking the height. One, a light thread is fixed to the end of an arrow, which is shot to the top of the rampart; the known length of the line determines the height of the wall. The other method relies on when the sun casts oblique shadows on the ground from the walls and the towers. The length of the shadows is measured, unknown to the besieged. A pole 10ft [3m] high is fixed into the ground at the same time, and the shadow it gives is likewise measured. It will then be easy to find the height of the walls, by calculating the relative length of one shadow to another, as it is known what height casts what length of shadow.[8]

Once the height of the walls was correctly judged, and therefore the length of the ladders calculated, the ladders had to be produced in quantity. Escalade was a game of odds – throw enough ladders against the walls of the fortress and at least some were bound to stick. Therefore they were produced in very large numbers; for the siege of Constantinople in 1453 the Turks used a total of 2,000 scaling ladders.

Climbing the ladders in action must have been a truly

► *This vivid artwork rather more accurately captures the poor life expectancy of the first men to climb the ladders. Archers at ground level were the best bet for suppressing the defenders. (World History Archive/ Alamy)*

terrifying business. The effort of climbing the ladders was enormous and it must have been awkward while gripping sword and shield ready for fighting at the top. Famously, one Sir Edmund Springhouse – an English knight – slipped and fell from a scaling ladder at the siege of Caen in 1417. Injured from the fall, he lay at the foot of the ladder. The French defenders, spotting the opportunity for cruelty, dumped burning hay on the helpless knight below, roasting him in his own armour.

Defensive response

The bleak example of Edmund Springhouse exemplifies how the defenders would have unleashed hell against an escalade attack. The attack would begin with multiple ladders being raised simultaneously across the fortress wall, with each ladder

▼ *This 15th-century civilian manuscript shows some of the options for scaling towers and walls, including a multi-section extendable ladder. (PD)*

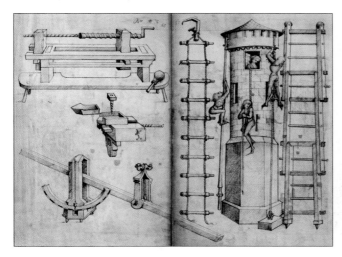

▼ *Here the defenders of Antioch used long poles to push the scaling ladders away from the walls, while huge masonry blocks smash both climbers and ladders. (PD)*

▲ A drawing of a wheeled shelter and integral covered boarding bridge by none other than the great Leonardo da Vinci (PD).

▶ A siege tower and boarding bridge, with troops crossing, feature in this image of the conquest of Jerusalem in the First Crusade (1099). (PD)

pushed into place by a long Y-shaped stick. The attackers would then move in single-file ranks to begin ascending the ladders. Burning oil, boiling water, quicklime, superheated nails, molten tar, boulders, baskets of rocks (balanced delicately so that if a ladder or attacker touched them slightly, they would tip out their contents), logs, hot sand (designed to work its way through the joints in a warrior's armour), plus arrows, javelins and slings, all rained down upon the climbers. Their best defence was simply to keep their shields above their heads and hope for the best, and also to rely on the efficiency of their own crossbowmen and archers who would fire rapidly at the battlements in an attempt to deliver suppressive fire. The defenders naturally attempted to push the ladders away, also by using Y-shaped sticks. Other ladder-clearing devices

included planks of wood hung off the battlements in the middle of long lengths of rope. The rope was drawn backwards and forwards, causing the plank to sweep across the face of the wall, dislodging ladders on the way.

The soldier who managed to get to the top of the ladder immediately faced bristling spears and swinging swords. If he could get past these, and if he was in the first ranks over, for a crucial few minutes he would typically be outnumbered on the battlements as the defenders crowded around him. Until sufficient attackers were up there alongside him, his chances of survival were low. Yet siege armies throughout our periods did take escalade to high levels of proficiency. For some, such as the Romans, escalade became almost the defining tactic of their practice of siege warfare; they optimised the tactics by launching surprise assaults, such as at night or when the bulk of the defenders were preoccupied with a religious rite or festival. As violent and unpredictable as it was, sometimes escalade was the only option.

◀ An image showing the construction of a bridge during the siege of Antwerp in 1584–85. The bridge was constructed across the Scheldt, cutting off the city's waterways. (Photo 12/Alamy)

SAMBUCAS AND 'SEESAWS'

Sieges produced no end of ingenuity when it came to depositing people onto contested fortress walls. Originating possibly in ancient Turkey, the *sambuca*, as far as we understand from the sources, was a counterweight device for depositing troops at the top of a wall. A long ladder or platform, possibly forming a type of covered walkway, was hinged unequally along its length to a high trestle platform, which was wheeled so that it could be pushed close up to a fortress wall. (There were also naval versions, mounted on ships for assault actions from the sea.) A counterweight on the short end of the walkway could be lowered to raise the longer end, enabling the men inside to get out and onto the battlements. The whole contraption was wheeled like a siege tower, to give it a degree of battlefield mobility. Another device was the 'seesaw', which worked on similar principles to the *sambuca* but without the counterweight. Instead, the soldiers inside the walkway moved from one end to the other, and passing the hinge point caused the elevated portion of the walkway to drop down in a seesaw-like fashion. Both the seesaw and the *sambuca*, however, are mainly encountered as theoretical propositions rather than historically documented tools of war, so it is unclear to what extent such devices were actually used in ancient sieges.

▶ *Siege equipment portrayed by Justus Lipsius, including a sambuca (bottom) and a seesaw-type lift for raising troops up the battlements. (PD)*

◀ *Reconstructions of a seesaw lift for troops and a mobile extendable ladder for escalade. Note the counterweight box for the lift. (Jordanet/ GNUFDL).*

▶ *A 15th-century seesaw boarding bridge from the text of German writer and fencing master Hans Talhoffer. (Det Kongelige Bibliotek/PD)*

SIEGE TOWERS

The siege tower is one of the most spectacular aspects of siege warfare. We have encountered the towers already in this book, as mounting platforms for battering rams and other engines. Yet the siege tower's greatest tactical application was as an elevated platform for depositing troops on top of high fortress walls or towers.

Siege towers were one of the most tactically striking and industrially intensive siege engines from the ancient to the medieval eras. The very largest specimens could be more than 30m (100ft) high, requiring herculean efforts and vast manpower both to build and to operate. During the siege of Rhodes in 305–4 BC, the commander of the besieging forces – Demetrius I Poliorcetes ('the besieger') – directed no fewer than 3,400 men to the role of pushing his great siege tower, although the realities of space around the tower meant that probably no more than around 1,200 men could be pushing at any one time. (See below for a more detailed description of this engine.)

TACTICAL ADVANTAGE

Given the massive enterprise required to manufacture and operate a siege tower, was the investment worth it? Based on the fact that they persisted in use for more than 3,000 years, the answer must surely be yes, although the rationale for constructing one must have been largely governed by the particulars of the individual siege. Tactically, siege towers offered several advantages. First, they provided a means to deploy a large number of soldiers right up to the fortress walls under protective shelter, thus reducing the attrition associated with open air movement. Second, they

▶ French troops bring up a siege tower during the siege of Château-Gaillard in 1204. This image illustrates how getting a siege tower up to the enemy walls could actually be one of the most difficult parts of the attack. (PD)

▼ An 18th-century engraving of wheeled siege towers and bridges used by Frederick II of Germany, Holy Roman Emperor, for the siege of Jerusalem, 1228. (PD)

THE SIEGE OF TYRE
The challenge of Tyre was that the fortress city sat on an island just off what is today the Lebanese coastline. Undeterred by the dividing waterway, Alexander deployed thousands of labourers to construct a 1km (0.6-mile) long rock causeway over the water. To provide fire support as construction continued apace, he deployed two huge siege towers at the advancing front of the causeway, from which various siege engines delivered counterfire against the defenders of Tyre. In response, the defenders sent out a fire ship to attack the causeway, and indeed the vessel succeeded in destroying both of the siege towers, despite their being clad in flame-retardant hides.

▶ A reconstructed siege tower with boarding bridge. Troops at the very top of the tower could provide suppressing fire as their comrades rushed across the bridge. (1bumer/CC-BY-SA-3.0)

▲ *The remnants of the Roman siege ramp at Masada (73–4 AD), built against the western face of the plateau for a giant siege tower to ascend. (Alamy)*

◄ *A slightly fanciful depiction of a monstrous Roman siege tower, c. 200 BC, complete with boarding bridge and battering ram. (Bildagentur-online/Alamy)*

offered a structure in which multiple other siege engines could be mounted and deployed to close range, where they were most effective. Internally mounted battering rams are common features in illustrations of siege towers, the rams either set close to the ground to attack the lower levels of the fortress walls, or high up to deliver smashing attacks directly against the enemy battlements. But siege towers could deploy a variety of weapons, such as *ballistae* firing through hinged ports on the face of the tower or catapults for launching incendiary weapons.

TRANSPORT OF TROOPS
The most valuable use of towers was as a mobile platform for directly assaulting the upper levels of an enemy fortress, especially via boarding bridges. Siege towers were built deliberately to match or exceed the height of the opposing walls, thereby taking away the enemy's defensive height advantage. As we have seen in this chapter, escalade was an unpredictable and bloody business; the assault capacity of each ladder was limited by the fact that the climbers could only ascend in single file. A large siege tower, however, could hold literally dozens of men, and keep them channeling up to the top via its series of internal ladders. In contrast to an assault ladder, furthermore, a boarding bridge could span the full width of the tower, thus in some ancient examples the bridge could have been 10m (33ft) square. If we take this as a theoretical example, and assume one man could occupy each square metre of bridge, then the bridge at any one moment could be transferring 100 men onto the opposing battlements in a matter of seconds, raising the possibility of overwhelming the defenders with high volumes of manpower. On this basis alone, siege towers were worth the investment.

Historical references to siege towers are very old indeed – and can be found in the late 3rd millennium and 2nd

millennium BC in Greek and Assyrian sources. It is during the second half of the 1st millennium BC, however, that siege towers emerge more forcefully in both narratives of sieges and also in technical and engineering documents. The Greeks and Macedonians were particularly skilful exponents of the siege tower, in both their construction and their tactical application. One of the most impressive demonstrations of their capability must surely be during Alexander the Great's siege of Tyre in 332 BC.

Siege towers were impressive works of carpentry and engineering. A sound primary source on the subject of their construction is Vegetius, who in his *De Re Militari* explains the basic principles of their construction and tactical application:

'Tower' refers to machines or buildings constructed from beams and planks, and covered carefully with rawhides and wool blankets, to protect the tower from enemy fire. Their breadth is in proportion to the height, for sometimes they are 30 feet [9.1m] square, sometimes 40 feet [12.2m] or 50 feet [15.2m], and height often exceeds that of the walls or the highest stone towers. By mechanical skill they are mounted on many wheels, by which means these vast bodies are put into motion. A city is in imminent danger when the siege tower is advanced up to its walls. For it consists of many stories, and contains various machines to be employed in the attack. In the lower part is a ram to batter the wall, in the middle, a bridge made of two parallel beams of wood and covered with a parapet of wicker, designed to be pushed forwards between the tower and the wall; the bridge then serves as a passage for the soldiers to attack the ramparts and enter the city. In the upper stories of the tower are men armed with long pikes, arrows, stones and darts, to clear the ramparts. One they gain this point, the city is their own. For what resource have the besiege,

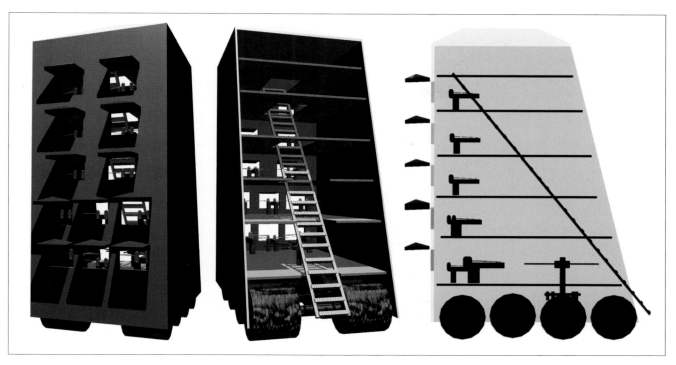

▲ A graphical representation of a Greek siege tower, showing a ladder ascent through the floors and hatch coverings for the fire ports on each floor. (Evan Mason/CC BY-SA 3.0)

▼ Tower of Demetrius I Poliorcetes during the siege of Rhodes in 305 BC, as depicted by the artist Friedrich Martin von Reibisch in 1842. (Heritage Image Partnership Ltd/Alamy)

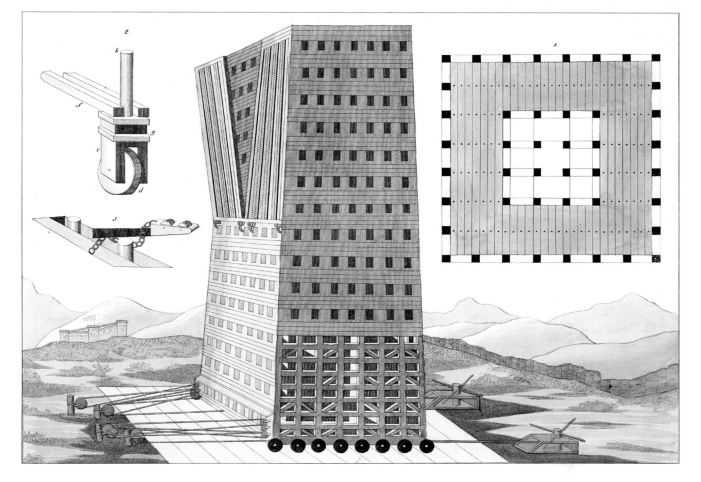

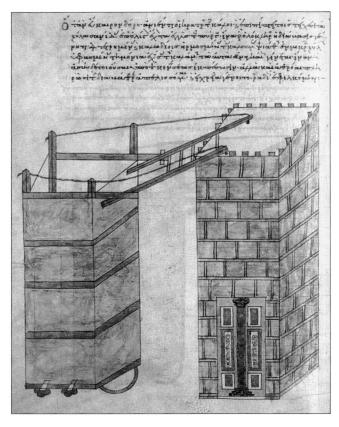

▲ *This siege tower in the* Poliorcetica *of Apollodorus of Damascus has a simple rope-lowered boarding ladder, a precarious prospect for those trying to cross. (PD)*

▼ *Drawing of a siege tower, from a 16th-century Italian copy of an 11th-century Greek manuscript of Hero of Byzantium's* Poliorcetica. *(PD)*

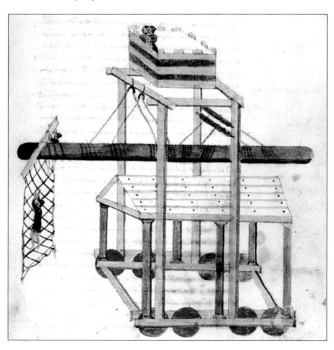

whose dependence was on the height of their walls, when they see the enemy suddenly raised so much above them?

DIMENSIONS

Vegetius's description provides us with many useful in-roads into the subject of siege towers. First, there is the issue of size. Siege towers could vary quite tremendously in their dimensions and weight, depending on factors such as the height of the fortifications they had to tackle, the number of personnel operating from within the tower, and the engineering capabilities (plus the availability of timber) within the besieging army. The basic mathematical principles governing the construction of a siege tower naturally meant that the greater the height, the wider the overall base and the dimensions and number of axles (if the tower was of a wheeled variety), for the sake of stability.

Useful outlines of the height–width ratios come from Diades, a military engineer who served Alexander the Great during the latter's great voyage of conquest across Asia. Diades of Pella was actually the former student of one Polyidus of Thessaly, who had provided Alexander's father Philip with some of the most formidable siege machinery of the ancient world. Diades was known for his improvements on siege towers, and he outlined two general sizes of tower for campaigns. The smaller, ten-storey version was 26.6m (87ft 3in) high and tapered from 7.5m (24ft 7in) square at the bottom to 6m (19ft 8in) square at the top, whereas the larger version was 53.2m (174ft 6in) high with 20 storeys, and working from 10.4m (34ft 2in) square at the bottom to 8.3m (27ft 3in) square at the top. The smaller version of the tower likely ran on four or six wheels, while the larger tower probably trundled towards its destination on eight wheels.

As we can see from the description of the larger tower, siege towers could be epic works of scale and industry. Indeed, the Classical and Hellenistic periods were eras of the *helepolis* ('city-taker'), siege towers that rivalled the greatest fortress towers for size and majesty.

THE HELEPOLIS

Developed during the 4th century BC by the likes of Demetrius Poliorcetes, Polyidus and Posidonius, the *helepolis* often climbed over 30 or 40m (100ft or 130ft) in height. Their scale enabled them to act as multi-function engines, mounting both siege artillery and walkways, the latter launched forwards to the enemy battlements through openings up the sides of the tower, covered by hinged shutters or flaps of animal hide. Each 'storey' would often consist of walkways and firing platforms rather than 'floors', connected by ladders snaking their way from top to bottom (there were designated routes for those ascending and those descending inside.) There is little doubt that even the smaller of such towers could leave a deep psychological imprint on all who witnessed them in action, as is evident in the following passage from Plutarch, who here describes the tower built by Demetrius Poliorcetes for the siege of Rhodes in 304–5 BC:

The quarrel between him and the Rhodians was on account of their being allies to Ptolemy, and in the siege the greatest of all the engines was planted against their walls. The base of it was exactly square, each side containing twenty-four cubits [11m]; it rose to a height of thirty-three cubits [15m – this appears to be an error, as the tower would have been about three times the length of the base], growing narrower from the base to the top. Within were several apartments or chambers, which were to be filled with armed men, and in every storey the front towards the enemy had windows for discharging missiles of all sorts, the whole being filled with soldiers for every description of fighting. And what was most wonderful was that, notwithstanding its size, when it was moved it never tottered or inclined to one side, but went forwards on its base in perfect equilibrium, with a loud noise and great impetus, astounding the minds, and yet at the same time charming the eyes of all the beholders.[11]

Plutarch focuses on the apparently smooth movement of the tower towards its goal, which if achieved was the something

▶ *A 19th-century vision of siege towers, amongst other siege devices. A siege tower ideally had to be taller than the outer curtain wall of the defending fortress. (PD)*

▼ *In this vision of the siege of Orléans in 1428, it is clear that the artist was struggling to convey the impression of a siege tower. (Gallica Digital Library/PD)*

to be lauded. The biggest of the *helepolis* weighed in the region of 160 tonnes, inching forwards on eight solid-wood wheels with nothing in the way of suspension, over frequently rough and rubble-strewn terrain.

MOVEMENT

Human muscle typically provided the motive power, although oxen were also used (such creatures were usually quickly killed or wounded by the defenders however). Many siege towers were simply pushed forwards, with dozens of men inside the base of the siege tower driving the engine forwards with their shoulders braced against the lower wooden framework. The pushing teams often needed some mechanical assistance, however. Pulleys might be used; the pulley wheels were emplaced ahead of the tower, and the ropes connected to the side beams while pulling teams drew on the other ends of the rope to each side of the tower. Alternatively, the tower might also have mechanical assistance built directly into the axles. For example, Polybius' *helepolis* designs included a large capstan, turned by 200 men, that applied movement to a drive axle through a continuous-drive belt.

DEFENSIVE RESPONSES

Regardless of the system of movement provided, getting a siege tower from point A to point B would have been a fraught business, especially while the defenders responded with their own series of countermeasures.

Logs and boulders would, if terrain allowed, be rolled down slopes into the paths of the towers, in an attempt to smash their wheels. Regular patterns of holes might be dug on the approaches to a fortress, forming a sort of inset concave minefield designed to destabilise towers. More cunningly, large earthen pots were buried into the earth as siege forces approached, with the top soil and turf replaced to disguise the embedded pot. When a tower wheel ran over the pot, the weight crushed it, causing a sudden ground subsidence that toppled the tower, or at least caused it to grind to a halt. The siege towers were also pelted with all manner of missiles

A SIEGE TOWER DESCRIBED

The siege of Constantinople in 1453 brought about a landmark event: the capture of the capital of the Byzantine Empire by the Islamic Ottomans of Mehmed the Conqueror. The siege ran 53 days from 6 April–29 May, during which time the Ottomans wielded all manner of siege engines, and constructed a mighty siege tower. Nicolo Barbaro, a chronicler of the siege, noted the rapidity of the tower's construction: 'On the eighteenth of May at night the Turks built a very fine tower in the following way. All through the night a great number of them were working away, and in the one night they made a tower built on the lip of the ditch and reaching higher than the walls of the barbicans, near a place called Cresca. This tower was made in such a way that no one would have believed that it could be done, and no work of this kind had ever been done by pagans before, nor so well constructed. In fact, I tell you, that if all the Christians in Constantinople had wished to build anything on such a scale, they could not have done it in a month, but these did it in a single night.' Barbaro goes on to note how the tower struck awe and fear into the defenders facing it. He also provides some illuminating technical details about how the tower was constructed and tactically deployed:

'The tower was built in the following way. First of all there was a framework of strong beams, protected all around with camel skins which covered it, and inside it was half full of earth, and with earth around it outside half way up, so that cannon or gunfire could not harm it, or crossbow bolts, and they had put hurdles outside and over everything else, with camel skins covering them; and they had also made a road to their camp, a good half mile in length, beginning from the tower, and on both sides of it, and over the top there was a double layer of hurdles and over them camel skins, so that they could go from the tower to the camp under cover without being in any danger from guns or crossbow bolts or fire from the smaller cannon; and the Turks inside the tower were excavating earth and casting it into the ditch, and kept on heaping up earth in this way. They heaped up so much earth that they overtopped the walls of the barbicans, and this tower was of great assistance to them in gaining the city. When the Turks in the camp had made this remarkable tower, and filled all the ditch with earth where it was necessary, they thought that they had made a great advance, and on this day nothing else happened at sea or on land, by day or by night. But, it is true, on this day the Turks shot a great number of arrows into the city from the place where the tower was, firing them, it seemed, from sheer high spirits, while our men were all very sad and fearful.'[12]

▼ *This high-quality model from the Kerak Archaeological Museum shows a siege tower with its side covered in overlapping hides. (H.P. Frei)*

from the defenders, such as catapult bolts and boulders. But the countermeasure most feared by those inside the towers was fire, either in the form of incendiary arrows or pots or through the application of flaming oil or Greek fire at close quarters.

In an unprotected state, a siege tower was in many ways little more than a mobile bonfire in waiting, being a structure of flammable beams with plenty of air circulation to encourage the development of flames. The typical defensive measure against fire was, as we have seen, to hang rawhides loosely on the outside of the tower, which were soaked with water to add to their naturally fire-resistant properties. Should a fire start to catch on the hides, water could also be tipped down the outside of the tower to dash the flames (the water was often held in sacks made from bullock intestines). The hides might also be formed into sacks filled with compressed wool or fabric, creating a shock-absorber effect to lessen the impact of missiles. Alternatively, bags of wet vegetation or chaff soaked in vinegar might serve the same purpose. There were a variety of other countermeasures. The woodwork of the tower could be coated with thick clay, and in more developed towers iron plating might be fitted to the three sides exposed to fire from the fortification, although this measure would dramatically increase the operational weight of the tower.

▼ *What appears to be a* sambuca, *depicted in an artwork by Hans Talhoffer. The front wheels would give some freedom in terms of positioning. (Det Kongelige Bibliotek/PD)*

SIEGE TOWER

This reconstruction of a siege tower shows a typical layout up to about the 14th century; before this time siege towers were more generally used as mechanisms for deploying boarding bridges, to attain the enemy ramparts. Once the tower had been pushed up to the wall and its wheels chocked in place, the tower could have held around 20–30 occupants.

1 Angled roof, to deflect missiles
2 Boarding bridge
3 Inter-floor ladders, with staggered access points
4 Structural beams
5 Main rear beams, typically used for pushing the tower
6 Solid wooden wheels.
7 Hide covering to guard against fire

THE BATTLE WITHIN

If a siege tower could fight its way close enough to the fortress walls, then a boarding bridge would be deployed. The construction of the boarding bridge could vary from a ladder-like contraption to a fully planked drawbridge. Deployment was either by ropes, pulleys or even by sliding the bridge out on rollers. Either way, the bridge had to be deployed quickly and the men who had to cross the perilous gap had to do so with focused aggression.

The siege assault was a spectacle to behold, with great siege engines and towers lumbering and thundering against the walls, men swarming like insects up siege ladders, dead and dying littering the base of walls on both sides, and missiles filling the air with whistling death. It is little wonder, therefore, that if attackers managed to enter a city, scant mercy might be shown the inhabitants. Ancient and medieval sieges regularly found their

final expression in some horrific massacres, with women and children often not spared, either from the blade or from a grim future existence as slaves in the conquerors' kingdom.

Some massacres have become legendary. In July 1099, after a one-week siege, the depleted and bitter Crusaders managed to break over the walls of Jerusalem, only by virtue of scraping together enough timber from the local area to make sufficient scaling ladders and two siege towers, one of which was burnt to the ground by incendiary defences from the battlements. Once inside the city, the European knights unleashed the most appalling slaughter on the inhabitants,

▼ *Kidwelly Castle in Carmarthenshire, Wales, survived the siege of Owain Glyndwr in 1403, although its gatehouse was set on fire. (CW Images/Alamy)*

women and children included. The number of dead is unclear, but it certainly seems to exceed 10,000. Several eyewitnesses report the knights wading through blood that was ankle-deep in the streets. The author of the *Gesta Frankorum* ('The Deeds of the Franks') recounted that '[Our leaders] also ordered all the Saracen dead to be cast outside because of the great stench, since the whole city was filled with their corpses; and so the living Saracens dragged the dead before the exits of the gates and arranged them in heaps, as if they were houses. No one ever saw or heard of such slaughter of pagan people, for funeral pyres were formed from them like pyramids, and no one knows their number except God alone.'

For the defenders, there were two main responses to the gravest of emergencies: 1) fight to the death; 2) surrender and hope for mercy. Vegetius was keen to encourage a sense of resistance from the besieged:

What the besieged should do if the enemy break into the city?

Many examples can be found of enemies who have been slain to a man, even after they had penetrated into a city. This will certainly happen, if the citizens continue

▶ *A chaotic scene at the siege of Acre, with Hospitalier Master Mathieu de Clermont defending the walls in 1291. (GL Archive/Alamy)*

▼ *A hinged scaling ladder. Speed was essential in assault actions, as the defenders needed to be kept in a state of disorientation. (Det Kongelige Bibliotek/PD)*

in possession of the ramparts, towers and highest parts of the city. The inhabitants, of every age and sex, might overwhelm the enemy with stones and weapons of all kinds deployed from the windows and the roofs of the houses. But the attackers, to avoid this danger, generally throw open the gates of the city, so that the besieged, finding that they have the opportunity to escape, may not be driven to a desperate resistance. The main recourse after the city is entered, either by day or by night, however, is to secure the ramparts, towers and all the highest places, and to dispute every inch of ground with the enemy as they advance through the streets.[13]

Vegetius gives sound advice to the besieged, and in doing so paints a picture akin to the urban warfare tactics taught in modern military units. Yet truth be told, if attackers managed to make their way inside a fortress, then usually the defenders had been already weakened sufficiently to have a limited capacity for resistance. Those who gave up their arms simply rested their lives on the mercy of the attackers, and that could be in very short supply.

6

DARK ARTS: SUBTERFUGE, SABOTAGE AND DIPLOMACY

The story of siege warfare is only partly about the use of weapons, physical assault and passive attrition. The outcomes of sieges were also often decided by cunning and negotiation, as well as by the efficiency with which both sides prepared for the action.

◄ *This highly formal representation of a medieval siege suggests that sieges were as much governed by culturally implicit rules as by military actions. (Getty)*

STRATEGIES FOR THE ATTACKERS

Sieges were decided not just by force of arms. Cunning, deceit, sabotage and psychological warfare also played their parts, often achieving the goals that weapons could not and even, on occasions, resolving a siege without any violence on either side.

It takes an act of deep imagination to picture the psychological forces at play during an ancient or medieval siege. Place yourself in the role of a subject within a besieged fortress. Your lord or commander has committed you, and your family around you, to resisting a violent enemy outside the walls. Food and water are running short, producing a fractious and desperate hunt for nutrition. Dead and wounded lie around you. A rain of missiles crashes down within the walls with terrifying frequency and power – you have witnessed entire dwellings pulverised in seconds by trebuchet stones. You know that sooner or later, if relief does not come, then the enemy will finally break through to within, most likely resulting in your death in a massacre, or a lifetime of slavery.

▶ *Such was the ferocious reputation of Mongol leader Genghis Khan (c. 1162–1227) that many potential enemies surrendered without any resistance whatesoever. (AwOiSoAk KaOsloWa; CC-BY-SA-3.0)*

▼ *The Holy Lance held by Adhémar du Puy before Antioch in 1098. Divine artefacts might convince a force of its sacred right to victory. (PD)*

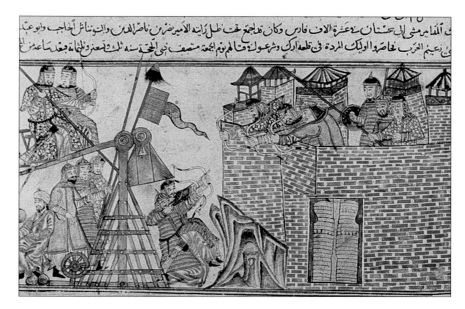

► *Mongol forces besiege a city in the Middle East during the 13th century. As a psychological strategy, the Mongols would often place prisoners captured in previous battles in front of their troops, to take the brunt of the enemy fire. (PD)*

Now imagine that the enemy, through a spy or skulking intermediary within the fortress, offers salvation to those who betray their lord, by turning against him or by surreptitiously opening the fortress gates for the enemy at an agreed moment. Not only do they promise clemency and freedom for everyone who betrays the fortress and its garrison, but they are even outlining a large financial reward – cruelly tempting to those whose lives often exist merely at subsistence level anyway.

What would you do? Of course, such hypotheticals are largely impossible to decide without the full spectrum of factors at play – human, political, military, social, cultural – and also without fear running through your bloodstream. But this scenario gives a sense of how suspicion and betrayal must have been constant companions during all but the most clear-cut sieges. The commander of a besieging army would have been vigilant for any and all opportunities to find human weak links in the defences, individuals who would turn against their masters to secure their own salvation or a political agenda. He must have lived in constant anxious vigilance, suspicious of every whisper in corridors and each small gathering in discrete rooms.

In this chapter, we will turn away momentarily from the study of the military aspects of siege warfare to the kinds of mental stratagems used by both sides for turning the battle in their favour.

NEGOTIATING TERMS

By far the best outcome for a besieging army was to take a fortress literally without a fight. A remarkably constant feature of siege warfare, crossing cultures and periods, is that the commander of the besieging army typically offered the fortress garrison or lord the opportunity to surrender before the fighting began. Even the most violent of armies, such as the Mongols of Genghis Khan, tended to operate by such rules, but the practice became heightened to the level of grand formality during the Middle Ages.

The offer of a non-violent surrender was a critical moment in the siege. Sometimes the negotiations would drag on for days or even weeks, as each side attempted to come to terms. If those terms ended in the surrender of the fortress, it was generally expected that the civilians and garrison would be treated humanely. If the fortress rejected the offer of surrender, then they were essentially giving up their rights to humane treatment should the fortress be taken, although

▼ *Assyrian soldiers verbally attempt to intimidate the defenders of Jerusalem in 701 BCE. Sometimes fear alone could compel a surrender. (PD)*

▲ *This 19th-century depiction of a siege in action illustrates how much industrial effort went into the production of siege engines and associated equipment. (PD)*

some medieval commanders still insisted on high standards of chivalry from their warriors.

Negotiations could also take place during the siege itself, once both sides had got the feel of each other and also developed a sense of the possible outcome. Messengers or heralds would be sent to announce the desire for negotiation. Such individuals, venturing out from or into the fortress walls once violence had already been unleashed, were in a precarious position. During the siege of Nesle,

France, in 1492, for example, the Duke of Burgundy sent a herald into the besieged fortress, to request negotiations with the commander, Petit Picard. Emotions were running high, and the herald was killed by the local people. Burgundy, incensed by this act, pretended that he wanted to persist in negotiating a peaceful surrender, but when the fortress finally sent out representatives to talk, the duke had them all hanged or beheaded.

Truce breaking

If a truce were conducted with restraint, however, it was generally agreed in the medieval period that all military activity – even the improvement of defensive positions – had to stop for the duration of the discussions. Yet these were rough times. Although the word of a commander or lord might be given as if inviolable, there were many instances of truce or surrender commitments being broken, a fact that could lead a fortress to default to resistance rather than surrender. Sometimes negotiations were broken in the most demonstrative fashion. During the siege of Acre in 1291, for example, the beleaguered Franks sent out messengers to the enemy commander, Al-Ashraf Khalil. Khalil was expecting that his opponents were bringing him the keys to the fortress – a classically symbolic act of surrender – but instead found that they wanted to agree terms of mercy for the civilian inhabitants of the city and to see if they could restore a previous truce. Khalil agreed to the negotiations, inviting the Franks into his personal tents. During the discussions, however, a sizeable trebuchet stone launched from inside Acre thumped into the ground near his tent. Khalil took this as a clear sign that all personal interaction was over, and the fighting resumed.

A more bloody instance of broken promises occurred during the siege of Baghdad in 1258 by the Mongol forces of Hulagu Khan (r. 1256–65). After two weeks of siege warfare, the Mongols captured the eastern wall of the city. Hulagau, sensing a weakening of resolve in his enemy, sent messengers through telling the garrison that if they surrendered they would be given safe passage. The soldiers obliged, but as they marched out they were rewarded by being massacred to a man. This brutality actually shocked the Arab commander, Caliph Mustasim, to surrender most of his court. They were taken into captivity, but the city's civilian population, who then felt they could now surrender themselves were, like the soldiers before them, subject to a merciless massacre.

INFORMERS AND BETRAYAL

When fighting was underway, the commander of a besieging force would be focused on the military tactics available, but would also keep an eye open for ways in which to introduce dissension and betrayal behind the fortress walls. If the

◄ *A besieging army would first issue terms of surrender to the defenders, the rejection of which would precipitate the military options. (Internet Archive Book Images)*

fortress was in a heavily populated area, the besieging army would often have the opportunity to familiarise themselves with the subjects of the local lord. These citizens could provide the commanders with information about the political and social tensions within the fortress, fractures that could be exploited by the besiegers.

Switching sides

Betrayal could be fostered by the besieging army via several strategems. There was outright bribery – the dangling carrot of cash or valuables prompting weaker members of the fortress to act on behalf of their enemies. Or the simple promise of food, freedom and immunity from vengeance might spur the wavering to become the unfaithful. Alternatively, the besiegers could let it be known that they might support a cause opposed to that of the fortress lord; on occasions, factions within a fortress might actually be more natural allies to their enemies than their own side. At the battle of Northampton in 1460, during the War of the Roses (1455–87), Lancastrian forces constructed a fortified camp, complete with rain-flooded moat, to resist the attacks of the Yorkists. Had the Lancastrians been unified, their chances of fighting off the enemy would have been good, but the disaffected commander of the left flank, one Lord Grey, decided that now was time to switch sides. Thus he not only failed to resist the Yorkist attack, but ordered his men actively to assist the enemy, giving them a hand up and over the defences.

▲ *At the siege of Centobrica, Spain, in 142 BC, the Roman general Metellus famously raised the siege in order to spare the lives of innocents. (PD)*

▼ *A contemporary illustration of the 'Lang Siege' of Edinburgh in May 1573, an action in which the town was mercilessly smashed by 10 days of cannon bombardment. (PD)*

▲ At the siege of Kufstein in 1504, the leader of the defenders, Hans von Pienzenau, is publicly executed by beheading. (INTERFOTO/Alamy)

Inside information

Once spies or collaborators were contacted inside the fortress, they could act in a number of different ways, such as physically opening the castle gates or actively leading the enemy to a secret entry point. Often the intervention could be subtle, although with equally devastating results for the fortress. In 1482 the fortress town of Alhama, Spain, was the objective of the Marquis of Cadiz and 4,300 of his men. The attack could have produced a prolonged siege – the fortress occupied a highly defendable piece of rocky high ground – but the marquis had spies in place inside the town, and they informed him of the times when the fortress was most poorly guarded during the night. In silence, a band of soldiers managed to conduct an escalade under the cover of darkness, making it over the walls and throwing the defending garrison into complete confusion. The castle was now under attack from both inside and out, and the enemy soldiers inside managed to make a breach through which their comrades could flood in. The fortress consequently fell after just a day's fighting.

If spies and traitors could not be found within a fortress, then they could always be introduced from without. During large sieges in which the siege lines were still loose enough for foraging parties to risk leaving the fortress for a time, soldiers

▼ The gates of Bordeaux are opened as the English capitulate to the French forces in 1453, during the Hundred Years' War. (North Wind Picture Archives/Alamy)

▶ *The Bakehouse Tower of Conwy Castle was partly destroyed by Parliamentary forces in the aftermath of a 17th-century siege. (Nigel Chadwick/CC-BY-SA-2.0)*

or spies from the besieging armies might be surreptitiously introduced into the group, entering freely into the fortress on the its return. One example of such cunning can be witnessed in 1401 at Conwy Castle, in North Wales. Henry IV (r. 1399–1415) had ascended the throne in 1399, and his ascension prompted a rebellion across Wales. Conwy Castle was a prime objective for the rebels, being a very powerful fortress that, because of its coastal location, could hold out for a extended duration against attack. Thus rather than opt for a direct assault, the rebels used duplicity to their advantage. At that time, the castle was undergoing renovations. Rhys ap Tudur and his brother Gwilym, cousins of Owain Glyndwr the leader of the Welsh rebellion, disguised themselves as humble carpenters and managed to work their way inside the castle on pretence of work. Once inside, they waited until the garrison was occupied with an Easter religious service, then killed the watchmen and opened the gates for a large group of rebels who stormed inside and took the castle. As was often the case in siege warfare, some lateral thinking could spare a lot of effort and bloodshed.

▼ *The view of Conwy Castle from the sea shows how natural defences were exploited by its builders. The fortress was taken by the subterfuge of Welsh rebels in March 1401.*

DEFENDERS' STRATEGIES

As well as being actively engaged in the military defence, the commander of a fortress during a siege was equally preoccupied in quenching dissidence, rebellion and betrayal before they could take hold. This was an activity that required inexhaustible vigilance and a highly suspicious mind.

Minor tensions in peacetime could become traitorous intent under siege conditions, so every individual and group within the fortress had to be monitored – the commander needed spies, even more than the attackers.

In fact, the critical element in guarding against sedition was proper preparation for the siege, putting in place measures that made the population inside more confident that they could survive the coming engagement, and ensuring that only the most stalwart and reliable men were in positions of command and influence.

Vegetius and Aeneas Tactics are superb sources for providing an insight into preparatory siege craft. Both of the writers implicitly recognised that the outcome of a siege might not be decided purely by military action, but also by more mundane practicalities and interpersonal relationships.

▼ *Carrigafoyle Castle in County Kerry, Ireland, was besieged in 1580 by English forces. Fewer than 70 defenders put up a futile defence against 600 attackers.*

STOCKPILING SUPPLIES

Sieges rarely came as a surprise to the besieged – the advancing enemy would be reported at least hours, but more likely days in advance. So, the fortress commander had a short window of time in which to make preparations for the coming ordeal. Most important was to stockpile food and other essential supplies, a fact that Vegetius explained in detail, noting that during times of conflict provisions of all types must be:

... gathered into the strongest and most convenient cities before the opening of the campaign. If the provinces cannot raise their quotas in kind, they must commute for them in money to be employed in procuring all things requisite for the service. For the possessions of the subjects cannot be kept secure otherwise than by the defence of arms.

These precautions often become doubly necessary as a siege is sometimes protracted beyond expectation, the besiegers resolving to suffer themselves all the inconveniences of want sooner than raise the siege, if they have any hopes of reducing the place by famine. Edicts should be issued out requiring the country people to convey their cattle, grain, wine and all kinds of provisions that may be of service to the enemy, into garrisoned fortresses or into the safest cities. And if they do not comply with the order, proper officers are to be appointed to compel them to do it. The inhabitants of the province must likewise be obliged to retire with their effects into some fortified place before the irruption of the enemy. The fortifications and all the machines of different kinds must also be examined and repaired in time. For if you are once surprised by the enemy before you are in a proper posture of defence, you are thrown into irrecoverable confusion, and you can no longer draw any assistance from the neighbouring places, all communication with them being cut off. But a faithful management of the magazines and a frugal distribution of the provisions, with proper precautions taken at first, will insure sufficient plenty. When provisions once begin to fail, parsimony is ill-timed and comes too late.[1]

Vegetius recognises that the preparations for war, and possibly sieges, are a truly civic affair; the population of both fortresses and surrounding areas were mobilsed to stockpile food and essential goods. In terms of sustenance, dried and durable foods such as flour, wheat, barley, dried peas and beans provided the foundations of the diet, while poultry, goats, cattle (if space allowed) and pigs were sources of fresh meat. The fortress interior required sufficient space to accommodate both the animals and their own fodder. If

▲ *The siege of La Rochelle (1572–73) saw the defenders receive some support, albeit largely neglible, from Queen Elizabeth I of England. (PD)*

such space was limited, then the animals might be quickly slaughtered and the meat salted to preserve it. For those fortresses on the coast, pans of seawater might be collected and the water allowed to evaporate, leaving quantities of salt behind for preserving. Fresh fruit and vegetables could be grown in gardens and boxes.

Water supplies were obviously critical. Underground cisterns, tanks and wells might be dug, especially in hot regions such as Palestine. In more temperate countries rain water would be collected in troughs and other receptacles, and guttering was often redirected to flow into tanks or wells.

Beyond food, many other items and materials constituted essential goods. Building materials such as quarried stone, timber and sheets of iron were invaluable for repairing siege-damaged buildings and defences and also for constructing defensive siege engines, if available in enough quantity. Incendiary substances such as asphalt and tar were stockpiled, as were stones for dropping from the battlements and arrows for the garrisons' bows.

▶ *The vast underground tanks at Masada, Israel, meant it was able to withstand seige for months. Water had to be stored in dark, cool places, to prevent contamination and evaporation.*

SIEGE TACTICS: RATIONING

Although resupply was possible once a siege was locked in place, the likelihood was that the encirclement would cut off all new provisions, so the fortress garrison and civilians would have to contribute food to the besieged community. Vegetius recognises that there might have to be some element of compulsion here, as not everyone might willingly contribute their personal stores of food to the common good. Aeneas Tacticus understood the same point in his reflections upon siege warfare: 'Furthermore, proclamations such as these are to be issued from time to time to frighten and deter conspirators: The free population and the ripe crops are to be brought into the city, authority being given to anyone so disposed to lead away or carry off from the country, without fear of punishment, the possessions of anyone who disobeys this regulation.'[2]

Once the stores were in place, they had to be strictly rationed and apportioned. Those who were to guard them had to be judiciously selected – people of firm character and self-discipline were required, as recklessness with the food distribution could quickly lead to shortages or even starvation, both of which loosened the bonds of loyalty. Ultimately, these individuals might have to harden their hearts in the face of the horrors that could accompany a siege. In some sieges, once food supplies reached critical levels only the fighting men might receive adequate rations, while the civilians were simply left to starve. This gave rise to the unedifying spectacle seen at the siege of Rouen in 1418–19. The city of 20,000 people, besieged by the forces of Henry V, was quickly reduced to eating vermin to survive, and some 12,000 of its citizens were actually expelled from the fortress to preserve the existing foodstocks. The English forces, however, were unwilling to feed the civilians, most of whom starved to death between the lines, hunkering down in utter misery in a ditch they dug around the base of the castle.

▲ King Henry V at The Siege of Harfleur in 1415. Although the English forces could access food from the surrounding countryside, much of it became contaminated in the summer heat. (Lebrecht Music and Arts Photo Library/Alamy)

▼ Charles VII of France besieges the town of Harfleur, held by the English. (Alamy)

▲ A twenty nickels coin issued by the Emergency Mint during the siege of Maastricht, 1579. (Artokoloro Quint Lox Limited/Alamy)

TRUST AND LEADERSHIP

Fortress leaders had to think carefully about who they chose to hold any position of responsibility, looking for chinks in their character armour that might make them more amenable to bribery and treachery. In the following passage, Aeneas Tacticus makes a circumspect reflection on the right people to take charge of manning the fortress gates – potentially the weakest point in the entire fortress:

> In the next place, no chance persons should be appointed keepers of the gates, but only discreet and sagacious men always capable of suspecting anything brought into the city; and besides they should be well-to-do and men who have something at stake in the city, that is to say, wife and children; but not men who, because of poverty, or the pressure of some agreement, or from other stress of circumstances, might either be persuaded by anyone or of themselves incite others to revolt. Leuco, the tyrant of Bosporus, used to discharge even those among his guards who were in debt as a result of dice-playing or other excesses.[3]

Here Aeneas Tacticus exhibits what we might call today psychological profiling. By selecting men who have families, the commander chooses those with something more at stake than merely self preservation. By studying their financial situation, it can be judged whether they might be susceptible to bribery. The example of Leuco is particularly telling, the tyrant looking into the very pastimes and leisure pursuits of his guards to dig up any signs of personal weakness.

▲ A contemporary song leaflet speaks of the siege of Vienna during the First Ottoman-Habsburg War (1526–55). (INTERFOTO/Alamy)

THE NECESSITY OF SIGNALS

Aeneas Tacticus outlined the importance of the besieged developing a private signalling system for guards and commanders, to help them to distinguish friend from foe. He also provides some historical insight into why this is important:

> As quickly as possible the besieged must be provided with signals, so that they will not fail to recognize those who approach them. For this is the sort of thing that has happened: Chalcis on the Euripus was captured by a fugitive operating from Eretria, aided by one of the inhabitants of the town who practised a stratagem of the following description. To the most deserted part of the city, where the gate was regularly closed, he kept bringing a firepot, and by keeping the fire going day and night he secretly one night burned through the bar of the gate and admitted soldiers at that point. When about two thousand men had gathered in the market-place, the alarm was hastily sounded and many of the Chalcidians were killed because they were not recognized, for in their panic they aligned themselves with their enemies as though they were their friends, each thinking that he was late in coming up. In this way, then, most of them perished by ones and twos, and the city had been in the hands of the enemy for some time before the citizens knew what was happening. It is necessary, then, in time of war, especially when the enemy is near at hand, first, that the forces which are being sent from the city on some enterprise by land or sea should be furnished with signals for use both by day and by night to those who remain, in order that the latter, if the enemy appear in the meantime, may not be unable to tell friend from foe. And, secondly, after their departure upon the enterprise, persons who will recognise the signals should be sent to watch, so that the men at home may get information of this kind while those returning are still a great way off. For it would be a great advantage to make preparations long beforehand for what is impending.[4]

▲ *Spanish conquistadors of Hernán Cortés massacre Aztec warriors defending the temple of Tenochtitlan in 1521, after a three-month siege. (Science History Images/Alamy)*

INTERNAL ESPIONAGE

In addition to being circumspect in selecting guards and other key people, the fortress leaders also had to put in place measures to make cooperative treachery more difficult. Any individuals under suspicion of disloyalty would be quickly arrested, and either incarcerated somewhere deep and inaccessible or executed. During the siege itself, anyone who showed the slightest evidence of desertion would generally be summarily executed, to dissuade others from following a similar path.

Aeneas Tacticus makes the point that gatherings of citizens had to be strictly controlled to prevent seditious ideas being circulated: 'The usual festivals are to be celebrated in the city, and private gatherings shall not take place, either by day or by night, but those which are really necessary may be held in the town-hall, the council-chamber, or other public place. A soothsayer shall not make sacrifice on his own account without the presence of a magistrate. Men shall not dine in common but each in his own house, except in the case of a wedding or a funeral feast, and then only upon previous notice to the authorities.'[5] During a siege, Aeneas Tacticus sees a breakdown in the division between public and private spaces, an emergency that requires the policing of all social and civic interaction. In a sense, during a siege everyone was suspect, and had to be treated accordingly.

BEYOND THE WALLS

Being relieved by external forces was the greatest hope of many populations under siege. The prominent social, political and military position of a fortress, and the generalised threat of an enemy rampaging through their lands, meant that allied armies might quickly come to the aid of a people under siege. But such was not always the case. Whether relief forces were sent or not was dependent upon many factors, not least whether the relieving army was confident that it could defeat the enemy in battle, especially once the besieging army had emplaced itself in defendable positions.

As we have seen earlier in our study, at the siege of Alesia in 52 BC, the Gallic tribes marshalled relief forces that were numerically superior to the Romans besieging the city, but three major attacks failed to overwhelm or dislodge them. In some cases, the besieged even accepted the futility of relief efforts. At the siege of Malta by Muslim forces in 1565, the defenders of St Elmo even sent out messages to friendly troops at Valette saying: 'Do not send further reinforcements, since they are no more than dead men', such was the overwhelming strength of the Arab onslaught. It should also be noted that the siege might well be just one of several campaigns going on within a particular territory – the siege of a single fortress could be the least of a country's problems.

Time

Time was also a crucial factor in the arrival, or not, of relief forces. To put together a major relief army could take days, weeks or even months according to the resources and will available, during which time the besieged might actually be defeated or compelled to surrender. Yet the besieged might also negotiate truces to buy more time for relief forces to arrive; here the passage of time could actually work in their favour, for passive attrition affected the besieging forces as well, potentially weakening them and making them less likely to resist the relief force once it arrived.

Communication

Once a siege was in place, the ability of the besieged to communicate with the outside world was extremely limited. The chain of enemy soldiers around the fortress meant that it was often impossible for couriers to slip out, unless the siege was loosely implemented or they knew some secret route. During the siege of Harfleur in 1415, for example, French messengers did manage to get through the English cordon to deliver requests for help to the dauphin, pleas that were unhelpfully ignored. Being such a messenger was also by no means a popular job. If captured, they were likely to be treated as a spy, i.e. brutally. During the Christian siege of Antioch in 1097–98 by the forces of Bohemond of Taranto, it became apparent that the Muslim defenders had many spies in the surrounding peoples, reporting on the Crusaders' strength and dispositions. The spies had the advantages of the multi-ethnic composition of the city, thus they could pass themselves off as Syrian, Greek or Armenian Christians (in some cases they actually were). As a countermeasure, Bohemond ordered that any spy should be roasted alive – the spy problem seems to have resolved itself quickly following the issue of this order.

A safer way to get messages to the outside world was to send them by courier pigeon. This system was certainly fast – far quicker than foot or horse – but it had its limitations. The first was that the message might not actually fall into the right hands, and therefore might possibly betray crucial information to the enemy. The second was that it might not arrive at all. The besieging army would typically be on the lookout for pigeons, and be ready to intercept with archers or with specially trained hawks. Finally, once starvation took hold, the pigeon might simply be eaten.

Assassination

Assassins were another option for the besieged to take the fight out beyond the walls, but they rarely seem to have been used or to have had much success. The only valuable object of an assassination attempt – the enemy commander or ruler – would typically enjoy high levels of protection and be surrounding by generally loyal men. Furthermore, during the medieval era knightly codes would often deem assassination methods as unacceptable behaviour. Yet attempts did happen. During the siege of Malaga by King Ferdinand II in 1487, a Muslim assassin, Ibrahim al-Gervi, managed to get close to what he thought was the king and his wife Isabella (who was accompanying Ferdinand on the campaign), and attempted to stab them. As it turned out, the opulently dressed couple, who were playing chess in their tent, were actually Beatriz Fernandez de Bobadilla, the keeper of the queen's wardrobe, and Alvaro de Portugal, brother of the Duke of Bragança. Alvaro was seriously wounded, but the assassin was killed, his body chopped into pieces, and the pieces hurled over the walls of the city in a grisly warning to all who might attempt such as action again. Such was the brutal psychology of siege warfare.

▼ *Roman troops led by the general Scipio Aemilianus take Numantia in 133 BC, finding most of the inhabitants dead or dying. (Chronicle/Alamy)*

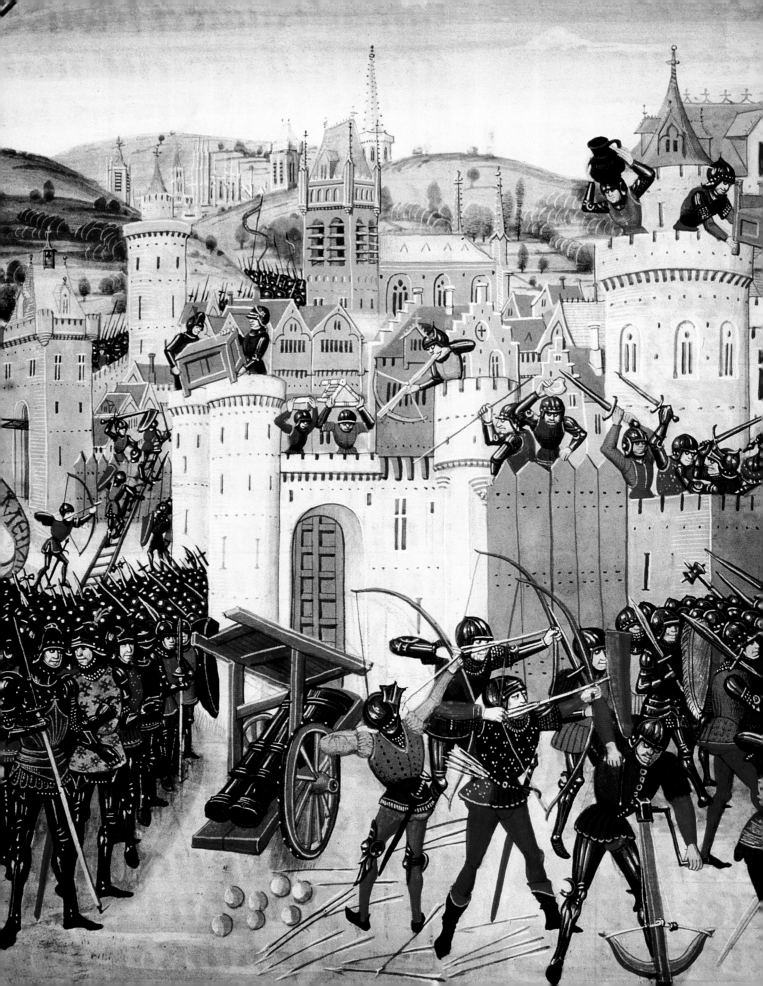

7

FIREPOWER: INCENDIARY AND GUNPOWDER WEAPONS

Gunpowder weaponry revolutionised siege warfare. Cannon steadily replaced the heavy torsion and counterweight siege engines of the past, as they came to offer a power, accuracy, range and reliability that exceeded potential-energy weapons. As the calibres increased, no fortress wall was deemed impregnable.

◀ *Early cannon were primitive affairs, as seen in the examples at the centre of this medieval siege. Note how the cart on which the two cannon are mounted has an early form of front shield. (Getty)*

WEAPONISED FIRE

In an age of mostly wooden structures, fire was one of the most feared weapons in siege warfare, used with great effect from both sides of the fortress walls. In the 14th century AD, a new destructive substance – gunpowder – entered military use in the West, leading to the invention of cannon, which transformed the principles and practice of siege warfare.

Although we tend to associate fortress construction with great blocks of masonry, wood was in many ways the principal building material. Most interior structures would have been entirely wooden or wood framed, and indeed many smaller and less expensive fortresses might actually have wooden curtain walls. Add in the prevalence of other combustible materials, such as thatch, coal, and cooking and heating oils, and it is little wonder that in the annals of siege warfare fire and incendiary weapons featured in some of the earliest narratives, as far back as the late 2nd millennium BC. Certainly, the ancient Egyptians, Assyrians, Persians, Greeks and Roman all utilised fire to a greater or lesser extent in their siege tactics, both as attackers and as defenders.

Incendiary warfare in an ancient siege could be a crude business, often consisting of little more than shoving or dropping burning materials onto or into the enemy fortress. In the following account, from Thucydides, we see the Peloponnesians under Archidamus resorting to basic fire tactics after attempts to build a siege embankment (the 'mound' referred to in the text) did not produce rapid results:

▼ *Fire weapons were used extensively in the siege of Jerusalem in 1099, including fire arrows, Greek Fire (see page 142–3) and bales of hay soaked in oil and wax. (PD)*

After this the Peloponnesians, seeing their engines availed not and thinking it hard to take the city by any present violence, prepared themselves to besiege it. But first they thought fit to attempt it by fire, being no great city, and when the wind should rise, if they could, to burn it; for there was no way they did not think on to have gained it without expense and long siege. Having therefore brought faggots, they cast them from the mound into the space between it and their new wall, which by so many hands was quickly filled, and then into as much of the rest of the city as at that distance they could reach and, throwing amongst them fire, together with brimstone and pitch, kindled the wood and raised such a flame, as the like was never seen before made by the hand of man. For as for the woods in the mountains, the trees have indeed taken fire; but it hath been by mutual attrition and have flamed out of their own accord. But this fire was a great one, and the Plataeans that had escaped other mischiefs wanted little of being consumed by this. For near the wall they could not get by a great way; and if the wind had been with it (as the enemy hoped it might), they could never have escaped. It is also reported that there fell much rain then with great thunder and that the flame was extinguished and the danger ceased by that.[1]

▶ *An ancient Chinese incendiary bird. The unfortunate creature would carry burning fireworks to the intended target; the fins on the arrows were intended to make the payload aerodynamic. (Jiao Yu and Liu Ji/PD-Art)*

▲ *Surrounded by caltrops, here are two Chinese incendiary grenades from the 10th–12th centuries. Each pot would be filled with a flammable substance. (Badseed/GFDL)*

This account raises on important environmental point about incendiary weapons; most of them could really only be effective in fine and dry weather. This notwithstanding, a large fire against the exterior of a wall could have a serious weakening effect on the integrity of the stonework. Indeed, during the medieval era sappers would sometimes emplace themselves at the base of a fortress wall, make an intensive fire and direct it against the surface of the wall with bellows, using the directed flame almost in the manner of an oxycetylene torch to degrade stone and mortar.

INCENDIARY ARROWS

One of the very earliest incendiary weapons was undoubtedly the fire arrow, which endured very late into history, even appearing in some accounts of 19th-century warfare in traditional societies, such as that of the Native Americans and some tribes of South America and Africa. At its most basic, the incendiary arrow consisted of a conventional arrow but with the shaft wrapped in twisted strips of fabric that had been soaked in a combustible mixture, such as resin, pitch or oil. All that was then required was to light the fabric and fire the arrow towards the target. This technique, when performed by dozens of archers simultaneously, could result in a veritable rain of fire on the target, whether that target was interior fortress buildings or a vulnerable siege engine. The only restriction on its practice was that the arrows generally required launch from loose bows at a high trajectory to achieve the range, limiting the accuracy – firing from a fully drawn bow produced a velocity and air flow that would generally snuff out the flame. Note that larger versions of the regular fire arrow could be launched by siege engines, such as the *ballista*.

Malleolus

Over time, the humble fire arrow developed into some more sophisticated forms. The Romans had a variant called the *malleolus*, which was fitted near the head with a small box

of open ironwork, which contained steel wire plus a highly incendiary chemical mix, such as a combination of sulphur, resin, oil and petroleum. Ammianus Marcellinus, a Roman soldier and historian writing in the 4th century AD, noted that such were the properties of the *malleolus* that water was insufficient to put out the spitting flames – only smothering the flames in sand was effective.

Falarica

Another fire arrow was the *falarica*, which featured an extended iron penetrating head that was coated with similar incendiary substances as those just described, secured with a wrapping of tow; on impact it penetrated deeply and burned intensively.

▼ *Various types of medieval arrows, including ones apparently mounted with explosive and incendiary charges, some possibly impact detonated. (Det Kongelige Bibliotek/PD)*

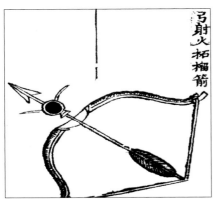

◀ *In this medieval Chinese artwork, we see a charge of gunpowder affixed to a standard arrow. The charge would be detonated by fuse or impact. (Yprpyqp/CC-BY-SA-4.0)*

GREEK FIRE

By far the most renowned of the incendiary compounds, however, was the legendary Greek Fire, which emerged most identifiably in 7th century AD Byzantium, although there are some hints that its existence might even date back to the 5th century BC. The exact composition of this fluid is unknown – mostly because the recipe was jealously guarded by those who possessed it – and likely varied somewhat in its ingredients list depending on the time and place. We can be confident, however, that it had a petroleum base, probably naptha crude oil or a similar product, to give its ferocious burning qualities; Byzantium's geographical proximity to the Middle East meant that it had ready access to natural petroleum products. Medieval writers note that Greek Fire was resistant to water; indeed the flames seemed positively encouraged by applying water. Only urine, vinegar and sand were reputed to be effective countermeasures. Such a characteristic suggests the addition of sulphur and maybe quicklime, but what fragments of recipes we have include various other concoctions, such as flammable tree resin.

Whatever the case, Greek Fire was certainly an extraordinary weapon, burning with a flame temperature of 1,000°C (1,830°F), with its violence in action made more so by its methods of deployment.

FUELS AND COMPOUNDS

As we have already seen, therefore, the efficacy of fire arrows could be improved by utilizing incendiary compounds. This in many ways is the continuation of the story of incendiary siege warfare, as the compounds grew ever more destructive over time. By the medieval period, military engineers had a broad spectrum of substances to choose from, and Konstantin Nossov has helpfully assembled a list of the most common:

> resinous tree; flax-tow (tow);
> resins, pitch, gum, rosin;
> turpentine;
> linseed oil; Ethiopian, aniseed, juniper, and 'brick' oils;
> sheep fat (melted);
> sulphur ('white,' 'red,' and 'brilliant') and 'sulphuric oil';
> egg yolks, 'egg oil';
> quicklime;
> petroleum;
> balsams;
> painting putty;
> wax;
> pigeon and sheep droppings.[2]

Each of these provided its own contribution to the fiery mix. Sulphur, for example, produced a choking and highly toxic smoke. Pitch, when added, gave the fire a method of adhesion to any surface. Oils enabled the fire to spread over a wider area, by flowing and splashing.

Projectors

Its most sophisticated delivery mechanism was basically an early form of flamethrower or projector, in which the burning liquid was ejected under the pressure of blacksmith's bellows from a brass or bronze tube, possibly up to distances of 15m

▼ *The fire lance was used to torch flammable structures during an assault or to repel defenders/attackers from a localised area. (Chronicle/Alamy)*

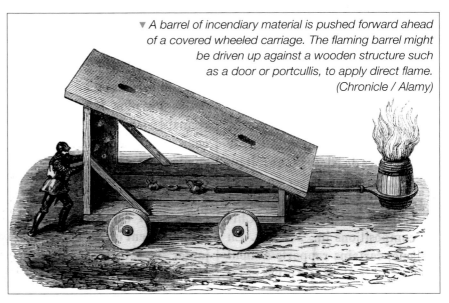

▼ *A barrel of incendiary material is pushed forward ahead of a covered wheeled carriage. The flaming barrel might be driven up against a wooden structure such as a door or portcullis, to apply direct flame. (Chronicle / Alamy)*

▶ *One of the earliest depictions of Greek Fire – the Madrid Skylitzes manuscript shows Greek Fire being sprayed over enemy ships from a metal siphon. (PD)*

(16yds). Some sources also indicate that the Greek Fire, in its liquid form, was heated in a pressurised caldron, the pressure adding to the flame's range and intensity once released. The projectors used aboard naval vessels were large and sophisticated affairs, but the Greek Fire projector was also available in a *cheirosiphon* ('hand-siphon') manportable version. This first of these appears in Byzantine sources in the 10th century, and its invention is self-credited to Emperor Leo VI the Wise (r. 886–912). The principal illustration of this system shows what appears to be a metal tube with a handle gripped by the soldier's left hand; he is firing the device by pushing in a plunger at the rear of the tube with his right hand, ejecting the flames from the other end in a manner similar to that of operating a huge syringe. Revealingly, the artwork shows Greek Fire being used specifically in the context of siege warfare, with the soldier directing the flame against a castle tower from his position atop a flying bridge.

The other method of applying Greek Fire – and indeed any incendiary mixture in siege warfare – was to throw (by hand) or hurl (by siege engine) the composition in a fragile receptacle, which shattered upon impact and released the flames or heated substance. Typical incendiary vessels, which were somewhat akin to early forms of hand grenade or mortar shell, were made of clay, glass, thick paper, leather or even tree bark. There were further innovations in medieval East Asia, such as ceramic containers filled with molten iron, and launched against the enemy from a trebuchet. Alternatively, the incendiary mix might be placed in an open iron cage structure, through which it burned in a manner similar to a World War II thermite incendiary bomb. One particularly interesting insight into the application of incendiary weapons comes from a medieval account of the siege of Montreuil-en-Bellay in 1147, in which the head of the besieging army, Geoffrey Plantagenet:

> ... ordered an iron jar, hanging from a strong chain, to be filled with the oil of nuts and the seeds of cannabis, and flax, and the openings of the jar to be sealed with a suitable

iron strip, firmly locked. Moreover he ordered the filled jar to be placed in a heated furnace for a long time until the whole thing glowed with over-great heat, so that the oil bubbling inside should boil. Having first cooled the chain by throwing water over it, it was taken out again, fixed to the arm of a mangonel and with great force and care, while it was alight, was thrown by the engineers at the strong beams of the breaches. It was expelled by the impact and a fire was made of the discharged matter. Moreover the overflowing oil joined the balls of fire, supplying food for the flames. The licking flames vomiting in an extraordinary increase, burned three houses and hardly allowed men to escape the fire.'[3]

By the 13th century, Greek Fire had spread well beyond the confines of the Byzantine Empire, and was found in use from East Asia (the Mongols are known to have had it in their arsenal) to Western Europe. This substance, along with the plethora of other flammable weaponry, made siege warfare a fiery and smoky business for both sides.

▼ *In this fascinating medieval image, a soldier on top pf a siege ladder launches Greek Fire onto a fortress tower from a portable hand-siphon. (PD)*

GUNPOWDER AND CANNON

Greek Fire may have added another dimension of terror to siege warfare but during the 14th century, a new pyrotechnic substance entered into the annals of warfare, one that fundamentally, over a period of time, changed the history of warfare, and indeed human history in general.

It is fitting that we bring this book to a close with the advent of gunpowder and cannon in the late Middle Ages. Gunpowder did not instantly revolutionise siege warfare, on account of the limited performance of early gunpowder weapons. But over time, as cannon grew in their power, accuracy, range and calibre, they initiated the inevitable obsolescence of castles and high-profile stone fortresses. The chemical energy of the cannon eventually came to offer a destructive potential far greater than the kinetic, elastic and gravitational energy offered by conventional siege engines. Furthermore, cannon eventually opened the route to the efficient mass production of standardised firepower, breaking free from the constrictions of materials and engineering skill needed to produce, say, a mighty trebuchet. The defining relevance of the cannon, however, was that it eventually rendered fortress walls largely impotent to being breached.

THE EARLIEST USES OF GUNPOWDER

The story of the cannon naturally begins with its source of power. Gunpowder – a composition of sulphur, saltpeter and charcoal – first emerged in China during the 9th and 10th centuries AD. Military technicians and commanders were quick to recognise its potential, given that it could burn fiercely when ignited as a loose powder but explode powerfully when detonated in an enclosed space. The East

Asian armies were particularly inventive when it came to applications for gunpowder weapons in siege warfare.

Directed delivery

Like the Byzantine and Middle Eastern powers, the Chinese armies were, by the 9th century, already heavy users of fire weaponry, including fire arrows, incendiary grenades and Greek Fire. Gunpowder, when it established itself, could be used either as a primary weapon or as an accelerant or power-amplifier for other devices. Paper packets of gunpowder were attached to arrows of varying size, tied into place with hemp and sealed with pine resin to form a semi-explosive missile weapon. 'Fire lances' were used – these were little more than a wooden haft with a what was essentially a huge gunpowder firework attached, typically described like a Roman Candle. Once lit, the roaring flame could be directed against siege ladders by fortress defenders, burning through the woodwork in short order, or could be used by attackers to suppress the enemy during an assault. The Chinese also became adept in launching batteries of gunpowder rockets from multi-launch rails.

Animals also have a long and sad place in the history of siege warfare, with foxes, dogs, cats, pigs, horses and mules all being used in various times and places as hapless delivery systems for flammable weapons. The Chinese, for example,

▼ *This Chinese gunpowder fire lance projects a blast of flame plus lead pellets as lethal projectiles. From the 14th-century treatise* Huolongjing. *(PD)*

▼ *A Chinese 'erupter' cannon, firing cast-iron gunpowder filled balls with an explosive shotgun effect. It must have been an unpredictable weapon to use. (PD)*

▼ *Another gunpowder weapon from the Huolongjing, here a multi-launch container for firework rockets, each tipped with an arrow head. (PD)*

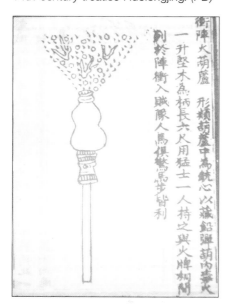

▲ *This cannon from Anping Fort in Taiwan is mounted on a suspension-less two-wheel carriage, although the spokes in the wheels at least indicate an attempt to lighten to overall weight of the gun system.*

tied small incendiary devices around the necks of birds and sent them flying into enemy fortresses and cities. One particularly horrific Chinese delivery method for gunpowder was to tie a large gunpowder bomb to the back of an ox, light the bomb fuse and also ignite an incendiary device on its tail, then send out the maddened animal into the ranks of the enemy attackers, in the hope of destroying siege towers.

Alternatively, gunpowder grenades were launched from simple throwers that used the springy properties of bamboo

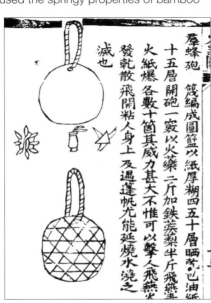

▶ *A hand-thrown Chinese bomb. The paper casing was filled with a charge of gunpowder mixed with metal pieces to form a shrapnel cloud. (PD)*

to create short-range throwing arms. In essence, these were the ancient versions of modern light mortars, and would probably have a range of between 50 and 100m (55–110yds).

Exploding devices

These weapons were just the tip of the iceberg when it came to Asian inventiveness with gunpowder. The 14th-century military treatise the *Huolongjing* ('Fire Dragon Manual') lists numerous different types or incendiary and exploding devices, from shrapnel grenades to self-detonating landmines, bombs that launched dozens of mini rockets to large mobile shields faced with fire lances to break up enemy formations.

Nor were the Chinese gunpowder weapons just on-paper curiosities, as is the case with some siege weapons, but were certainly used in action on many occasions. In 1132, during the Jin-Song Wars, Jin forces besieged the city of De'an, and used siege towers with 'sky bridges' to assault the fortress walls. The defenders, led by Chen Gui, the city prefect, used not only fire lances to repel both the siege towers and escalade – the first use of fire lances in recorded history – but also launched explosive gunpowder bombs at the enemy both by hand-thrown and engine-launched means, and even managed to destroy some of the siege towers

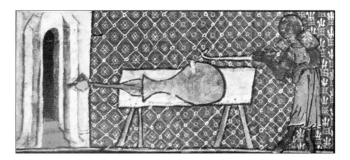

▲ *Walter de Milemete's illustration of one of the earliest bell-shaped cast cannon, the projectile was a huge dart padded at the rear of the shaft. (PD)*

with the ghastly oxen bombs. Such was the intensity of the combusting and explosive onslaught that eventually the Jin were forced to retreat.

Another important step forwards in Chinese explosive weaponry were the *zhen tian lei*, or 'thundercrash bombs', which were gunpowder-filled grenades fully encased in bottle-shaped iron containers. Introduced during the 13th century, the thundercrash bombs delivered serious explosive and fragmentation effects, being used in actions such as the Jin's defence of Hezhong against the Mongols in 1213. The medieval Chinese also investigated the potential of poisonous gas and caustic smoke in their incendiary and explosive weapons, mixing gunpowder with various noxious and irritant compounds to choke or blind their enemies.

The formula for gunpowder eventually crept its way out from East Asia, through the Middle East, and entered Western Europe during the 12th or 13th century. In the West, we do not see so much of the almost playful inventiveness of the Chinese in developing gunpowder weaponry. Instead we witness the application of gunpowder for its properties as a propellant in tubular missile weapons, and especially the cannon.

CANNON

We should not see the cannon as a purely Western innovation. Cast-iron cannon-type weapons had emerged in China by the 13th century; indeed, the earliest specimen of a gunpowder firearm in history dates back to 1288, and is of Chinese origins. During the 14th century, both China and Korea were utilising cannon in siege warfare, and it was during this century that we also see Western powers applying the cannon to siege warfare.

The earliest illustration of a cannon in the West is that shown in the English manuscript *De nobilitatibus, sapientiis, et prudentiis regum*, written in 1326 by the English scholar Walter de Milemete on the commission of Queen Isabella. One marginal illustration shows a *pot de fer*, a prototype muzzle-loading cannon of cast bronze, shaped like a huge vase resting horizontally on a trestle, firing a large arrow from the neck of the vase as the operator applies a linstock to a vent hole at the rear. The shape of this gun was a quickly passing phase, and is likely explained by applying the already prevalent skills of casting bells to the manufacture of weaponry. The straight-barrelled cannon soon established its dominance, however, and although there were some early breech-loading examples it was the muzzle-loading variety that would be the primary design of gunpowder artillery for the next 500 years.

Technical developments

This book, focused as it is on siege warfare, is not the place to present a detailed history of the evolution of cannon during the medieval period. Suffice to say that in Western Europe during the 14th and 15th centuries, the designs of cannon barrels were developed in their material and constructional strength to enable them to fire heavier balls over longer distances. The early barrels, made from longitudinal strips of iron welded together and reinforced by lateral hoops, were replaced by solid one-piece weapons cast in bronze or iron (therefore less liable to explode under pressure).

Trial and error featured much in cannon metallurgy and construction, and the early weapons were almost as dangerous to the user as they were to the enemy. Yet the design of cannon had to keep pace with developments in the formulation of gunpowder, which made a significant jump forwards in the 15th century with the introduction

◄ *A 1529 German manual on gunpowder weaponry. Operating unreliable early cannon was extremely dangerous to gunners. (Chemical Heritage Foundation/PD)*

► *A mighty Ottoman cannon used during the siege of Constantinople in 1453, displayed in The Military Museum, Istanbul. (Cüneyt Türksen/PD)*

MEDIEVAL SIEGE CANNON

This early cannon is fitted to a rudimentary wooden cradle, with elevation brackets at both the front and rear of the piece. Note how there is no system of recoil control whatsoever; it was not uncommon for wooden cradles to split apart during prolonged firing. Traverse was a matter of manhandling the entire structure into the intended direction of fire.

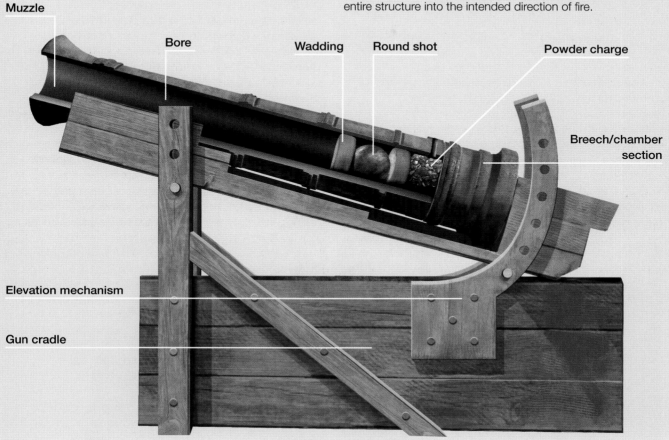

Muzzle

Bore

Wadding

Round shot

Powder charge

Breech/chamber section

Elevation mechanism

Gun cradle

of 'corned powder' – the gunpowder was formed into small grains that ensured a consistent distribution of the constituent ingredients, and therefore made the powder more dependable and powerful. In terms of mounts, the very first cannon were simply clamped onto basic trestles or carts. Later they came to sit upon mobile wheeled carriages, and over time the carriages themselves grew more sophisticated, including the ability to control elevation and traverse. Recoil control, however, was either rudimentary or, more typically, non-existent, and in most cases during the early Middle Ages manoeuvring the cannon into position for firing was a back-breaking and imprecise business.

Cannon design

Cannon came to be designated in a variety of sizes based on calibre. In Western medieval siege warfare, the most significant cannon were the largest of these types, known as

▼ *A huge bombard mortar used by the Knights of St John of Jerusalem in the 15th century. Such cannon were purely high-trajectory, short-range weapons. (PHGCOM/GFDL)*

'bombards', emerging in the late 14th and 15th centuries. These were real monsters, many metres in length, weighing often tens of thousands of kilograms and with cavernous calibres. The infamous 'Mons Meg' that graces Edinburgh Castle is one particularly well-known example.

Built in 1449 on the orders of Philip the Good, Duke of Burgundy, Mons Meg was eventually sent to service with James II, King of the Scots, in 1454, after which it saw service as a siege weapon until its barrel burst in 1680. It weighed 6.9 tonnes (6.8 long tons) and measured 4.6m (15ft 1in) in length. Its calibre was an astonishing 510mm (20in), making it one of the largest cannon in history, by calibre. Although cannon progressively switched to fire solid iron shot in the 15th and 16th centuries, stone ammunition – sometimes lead covered to protect the cannon's bore – was the typical shot of the bombards. Mons Meg could hurl a sandstone or granite ball weighing up to 170kg (375lb) for a distance of about 3km (1.9 miles), unleashing extraordinary destructive effect on both masonry and stone buildings. Mons Meg was far from alone in the world of mighty siege cannon. Other specimens included a cast bronze Turkish specimen measuring more

than 5m (16ft 5in) in length and with a calibre of 63.5cm (25in), and a Russian brute of similar length but weighing 40,000kg (88,184lb) and with a calibre of 89cm (35in).

USE IN ACTION

Cannon were extremely expensive to manufacture and use, and were therefore only accessible in large numbers to rulers or commanders with deep pockets. This was not just a matter of manufacturing costs – cannon also came with their own long list of logistical demands. A single bombard alone could require about 24 horses simply to draw it to the site of the siege. Then there was all the kit that came with it

▼ *This medieval cannon shows how the barrel was made from wrought-iron hoops; the hoops were put in place straight from the blacksmith's forge. As they cooled, they tightened up to strengthen the barrel. (Toxophilus/CC-BY-SA-3.0)*

– powder, shot (stone masons would often also manufacture shot at the siege location), rope, firing and loading tools. Historian Christopher Gravett explains that 'In 1477 two Italian bombards required 48 wagons each with two or four horses to transport the tiller, gunpowder, shot and equipment. Bridges and roads sometimes needed reinforcement, and large guns were often taken by river as an easier alternative.'[4]

In addition to the logistical burden, the siege commanders also had to ensure that they had sufficient men trained in the use of the new weapons, not always an easy matter in the days before the establishment of official engineer and artillery units in the many armies. Firing a cannon, and using it to best effect, required personnel who knew what they were doing. In the following passage, an eyewitness to the siege of Constantinople in 1453, Hermodoros Michael Kritovoulos, explains the firing method of the Turkish guns, which broadly applies to all cannon of the era:

> And now I will speak of its method of working. First, what is called 'fodder' [powder] was put in, filling up tightly the rear compartment and cavity of the machine up to the opening of the second compartment which was to receive the stone cannonball. Then there was put in a huge rod of strongest wood, and this, pounded hard by iron bars, pressed down on the material inside, closing in and packing down the powder so completely that, whatever happened, nothing could force it out in any way except by an explosion. Then they brought the stone also, pushing it in until they used the rod and fitted the stone in snugly on all sides. After this, having pointed the cannon torwards whatever it was

◄ *This 16th-century European cannon was known as the 'Elephant of King Matthias'. It is fully mobile, set on a four-wheel carriage. (PD)*

intended to hit, and having levelled it by certain technical means and calculations towards the target, they brought up great beams of wood and laid them underneath and fitted them carefully. On these they placed immense stones, weighting it down and making it secure above and below and behind and everywhere, lest by the force of the velocity and by the shock of the movement of its own emplacement, it should be displaced and shoot wide of its mark. Then they set fire to it through the short hole behind, igniting the powder. And when this took fire, quicker than it takes to say it, there was a fearful roar first, and a shaking of the earth beneath and for a long way off, and a noise such as never was heard before. Then, with an astounding thunder and a frightful crashing and a flame that lit up all the surroundings and then left them black, the rod, forced out from within by a dry hot blast of air, violently set in motion the stone as it came out.[5]

Risks

The step-by-step simplicity of this description belies the complexity of the physics and the skill set required to operate cannon safely (for the users). Take the issue of powder and shot weights. Too much propellant with too heavy a shot could literally rip open a cannon barrel with explosive effect, killing all those around them. Too little propellant, and the ballistic performance of the cannon would be poor – instead of flying hundreds of metres, it might simply skip a few dozen metres along the ground. The gun team also had to get to grips with numerous technicalities, including factors such as the differing performances of the cannon in wet and dry conditions, how to avoid spontaneous detonations while reloading a hot barrel, how to cope with the recoil (some of the largest bombards could fire barely ten rounds a day, such was the harsh effect of recoil on gun and mount) and how to calculate trajectory by applying appropriate elevation.

Effect on target

As history now knows, the investment of time, energy and manpower was deemed to be worthwhile in the end. Hermodoros Michael Kritovoulos here continues his account, explaining the effect of the cannon projectile on the target:

And the stone, borne with tremendous force and velocity, hit the wall, which it immediately shook and knocked down, and was itself broken into many fragments and

◄ *A cast-iron cannon ball, 63mm (2.4in) in diameter, weighing 820g (2lb). (Portable Antiquities Scheme/CC-BY-SA-2.0)*

▲ *Cannon also enhanced the firepower of defensive positions. Here we see the Gun Deck on Portland Castle in Dorset, a coastal fortress built by Henry VIII in the early 1540s.*

▲ *A 15th-century woodcut shows wheeled cannon being fired at the battlements of a castle, with the round shot smashing the upper defences. (Chronicle/Alamy)*

scattered, hurling the pieces everywhere and killing those who happened to be near by. Sometimes it demolished a whole section, and sometimes a half-section, and sometimes a larger or smaller section of a tower or turret or battlement. And there was no part of the wall strong enough or resistant enough or thick enough to be able to withstand it, or to wholly resist such force and such a blow of the stone cannonball. Such was the unbelievable and inconceivable nature of the power of this implement. Such a thing, the ancients, whether kings or generals, neither had nor knew about. Had they possessed it, nothing could have withstood them at all, nor stood up against them in their sieges; nor would it have been difficult for them to topple over and destroy walls. Even the best fortified of them would have offered no obstacle. They built walls, and dug entrenchments, and mined under the earth, and did all sorts of other things so as to secure possession of cities and capture forts, but all these would have surrendered quicker than it takes to tell it, if shattered and overthrown by these machines. But they had none.[6]

IMPACT ON SIEGE WARFARE

Here was the core reason why cannon had such a revolutionary effect on siege warfare. Torsion or counterweight artillery could and did bring down fortress walls, as we have seen, but their power constraints meant that their ability to punch through solid stone was unpredictable. Cannon brought with them a *predictable* ability to create breaches in a fortress, once early issues with powder, barrel strength and reliability were brought under control. The predictability came largely from the fact that cannon offered a largely repeatable trajectory (depending of course on the gunners' ability to

reposition the gun accurately after each shot), which meant the same section of wall could be smashed in the same place time and time again, and with highly directed force (cannon offered a flatter trajectory than trebuchets, often amounting to what we today call direct fire), eventually producing a breach. Because of this quality, cannon brought about a revolution in siege warfare, because the fortress itself now appeared to offer just temporary shelter, rather than – if defended properly – an unyielding bastion.

Fortress design responded accordingly to the new threat, of course. Castle locations became lower, acknowledging the

▼ *This 15th-century illumination is interesting as it shows a double cannon cradle. Such an arrangement was quickly abandoned. (PD)*

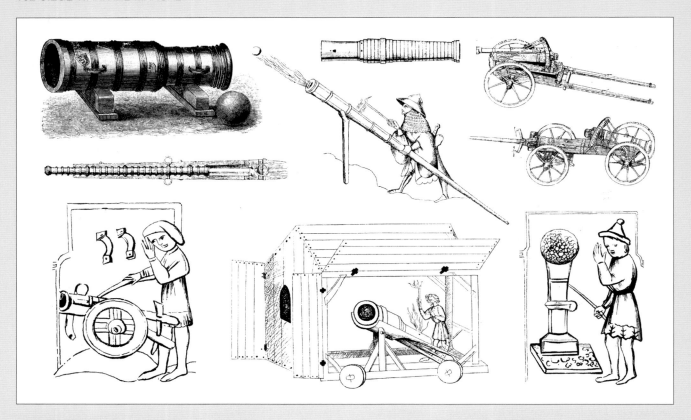

SIEGE TACTICS: COUNTERFIRE

Once cannon and gunpowder weaponry arrived on the scene, they were used by both besieging forces and defenders – this was not a one-sided technology. A classic illustration of this fact is the siege of Malta in 1565, the island, defended by the Knights Hospitaller, was under seige by the Ottoman Turks. The Turks, as we shall see, were early adopters and enthusiastic users of early cannon, and brought with them to the battle more than 65 siege guns, from which they would fire an estimated 13,000 pieces of shot throughout the siege. At times the Turkish fire resembled the rolling barrages of World War I in intensity and ferocity. One aspect of this fire became clear – the Turks could use the new weapons to breach walls almost at will. The historian Jim Bradbury notes this fact regarding the action around the

▲ A vintage engraving shows a selection of early pieces of gunpowder artillery, from bamboo cannon to more developed cast-iron pieces. (gameover/Alamy)

island's Fort St Michael, but also switches to acknowledge to the power of the defensive cannon fire: 'The bombardment on St Michael's began from the batteries established on nearby heights. Again the effect was murderous, showing the great impact of cannon by this period; part of the wall soon collapsed. The Turkish cannon power at Malta was probably greater than at any other siege we have witnessed. The impact of the weapon can hardly be better illustrated; breaches were made every time the Turks set up a new major battery, yet breaches do not always win sieges. It must be noted that the fire of the defenders, using guns from prepared positions behind the protection of walls, was even more murderous: more Turks died at Malta by far than Christians.'[7] The Christian defensive fire was certainly used flexibly and devastatingly. Coastal batteries wiped out approaching Turkish ships. Matchlock muskets cut down enemy infantry attempting to scale walls. On one occasion, a Turkish siege tower, approaching the defensive walls, was blasted to destruction by a cannon at close range using chain shot; the Knights hid a cannon muzzle behind an opening in the wall, then unveiled the barrel to the shocked attackers once they had entered into range.

◄ Bombards had to be placed close to defences to be effective, bringing its crew under the fire of hand-held weapons. (© BrokenSphere/Wikimedia Commons)

▶ *Old stone cannon ballls litter the ground around the walls of medieval Jerusalem, testimony to the intensity of fire that could be generated. (Mattes/PD)*

fact that cannon perform at their best when angled upwards at a higher target (the upward angle of the gun barrel ensures that the ball is better seated on the powder charge). Walls became even thicker, and sharp angles were avoided in favour or sloped faces and rounded towers, which deflected shot rather soaked up the impact. Platforms were built to mount cannon internally as defensive weapons, and we also start to see the appearance of musket loops in battlements and towers.

Setting the future

Here, in essence, is the situation that would take our story of siege warfare up to the present day, if that were our remit. Fortifications and fortresses would remain important well into the 20th century, although the low-profile cupolas and pillboxes of modern fortifications such as those at Eben Emael or the Maginot line are a world away from towering keeps and curtain walls. Fortifications toughened even further, evolving into hardened ferro-concrete and steel labyrinths, but their priority became staying low and flat, reinforced by surrounding earth and with much of their operational space underground. Out went the long defensive walls, and in came fieldworks. Now the outcome of a siege was decided by

firepower, the defender's 'walls' being the bullets and shells that blunted attacks. Starvation, endurance and other forms of passive attrition still played a key role in siege warfare – think the siege of Leningrad in World War II – but the days of escalade, towers, mighty siege engines and towering castles had largely passed by the 18th century.

▼ *French troops of Charles VIII, with horse-drawn and wheeled artillery of standardised design, enter Naples in the year 1495. (CC-PD-Mark)*

ENDNOTES

CHAPTER 1

1. Nossov 2006: 233
2. Thucydides: 6.98.2–4
3. Campbell 2005: 11
4. Caesar 7.69–74
5. Horrox 1994: 17

CHAPTER 2

1. Vitruvius 10.13.1–2
2. Vitruvius 10.13.4–6
3. Vitruvius 10.15.1–7
4. Nossov 2006: 101
5. Thucydides 2:76
6. Adapted from Vegetius 4.23

CHAPTER 3

1. Campbell 2003a: 12
2. 'Translation of Cheiroballistra': http://ballista.wikia.com/wiki/Translation_of_Cheiroballistra
3. Nossov 2006: 149
4. Procopius 5.21.103–05
5. Procopius 5.23.118
6. From *Auctarium Aquicinense*, translated by Bill Zajac at: http://www.deremilitari.org/RESOURCES/SOURCES/ascalon.htm
7. Nicolle 2002: 36

CHAPTER 4

1. De Vries 1992: 133–34
2. Nicolle 2003: 13
3. Nicolle 2003: 13
4. Nicolle 2002: 15–16
5. Sibly 1998. Extract taken from: http://deremilitari.org/2014/04/the-siege-of-termes-1210-according-to-the-historia-albigensis/ Reprinted by permission of Boydell & Brewer Ltd
6. Bradbury 1992: 268
7. Nicholson 2017: e-book
8. Matheson 2011: 645

CHAPTER 5

1. Wiggins 2003: 38
2. Polybius 21.28 [*Histories*]
3. Aeneas Tacticus 37.1–9
4. 'The Siege of Constantinople in 1453, according to Nicolo Barbaro': accessed at http://deremilitari.org/2016/08/the-siege-of-constantinople-in-1453-according-to-nicolo-barbaro/ – taken from Melville-Jones 1969.
5. Nossov 2003: 119
6. Campbell 2005: 11
7. Campbell 2005: 12
8. Adapted from Vegetius 4.30
9. Adapted from Vegetius 4.17
10. Campbell 2003b: 6
11. Plutarch, Demetrius: 241
12. 'The Siege of Constantinople in 1453, according to Nicolo Barbaro'
13. Vegetius 4:25

CHAPTER 6

1. Adapted from Vegetius 3.3
2. Aeneas Tacticus 10.3
3. Aeneas Tacticus 5.1–2
4. Aeneas Tacticus 4.1–6
5. Aeneas Tacticus 10.4–5

CHAPTER 7

1. Thucydides 2.77.1–6
2. Nossov 2003: 192–93
3. Quoted in Nicolle 2002: 41
4. Gravett 1990: 54
5. 'The Siege of Constantinople in 1453, according to Kritovoulos': http://deremilitari.org/2016/08/the-siege-of-constantinople-in-1453-according-to-kritovoulos/ – taken from *History of Mehmed the Conqueror by Kritovoulos* (1954).
6. Ibid.
7. Bradbury 1992: 238

BIBLIOGRAPHY AND FURTHER READING

PRIMARY SOURCES

Aeneas Tacticus – *Aineiou Poliorketika. Aeneas on Siegecraft Hunter* (1927). Prepared by L.W Hunter, revised by S.A Handford. Oxford: Clarendon Press.

Caesar – *Caesar's Gallic War* (1869). Trans. by W.A. McDevitte. New York: Harper & Brothers

Heron of Byzantium – *Two Tenth-Century Instructional Manuals by 'Heron of Byzantium'* (2000). Compiled and trans. by Denis F. Sullivan. Washington DC: Dumbarton Oaks Studio.

Itinerarium Peregrinorum Et Gesta Regis Ricardi – The Chronicle of the Third Crusade: The Itinerarium Peregrinorum et Gesta Regis Ricardi (2001), Trans. by Helen J. Nicholson. London: Routledge

Kritovoulos – *History of Mehmed the Conqueror by Kritovoulos* (1954). Trans. by Charles T. Riggs. Princeton, NJ: Princeton University Press.

Nicolo Barbaro – *Diary of the Siege of Constantinople 1453* (1969). Trans. by John Melville-Jones. New York: Exposition Press.

Peter of les Vaux-de-Cernay – *The History of the Albigensian Crusade: Peter of les Vaux-de-Cernay's Historia Albigensis* (1998). Trans. by W.A. and M.D. Sibly. Woodbridge: Boydell & Brewer.

Philo Mechanicus – *Philo Mechanicus: On Sieges* (2016). Trans. by David Whitehead. Stuttgart: Franz Steiner Verlag.

Plutarch – *Plutarch's Lives: The Dryden Plutarch* (1910). E. by Ernest Rhys. London: J.M. Dent

Polybius – *Histories* (1889). Trans. by Evelyn S. Shuckburgh. London, New York: Macmillan.

Procopius – *Procopius of Caesarea: History of the Wars Books V and VI – The Gothic Wars* (1919). Trans. by H.P. Dewing. London: William Heinemann; Cambridge, MA: Cambridge University Press.

Thucydides – *The Peloponnesian War* (1910). Trans by Richard Crawley. London: J. M. Dent; New York: E.P. Dutton.

Vegetius – *Military Institutions of Vegetius* (1767). Trans. by Lieutenant John Clarke. London: W. Griffin.

Vitruvius – *The Ten Books on Architecture* (1914). Trans. by Morris Hicky Morgan. Cambridge: Harvard University Press; London: Humphrey Milford; Oxford: Oxford University Press.

SECONDARY SOURCES

Bradbury, Jim (1992). *The Medieval Siege*. Woodbridge, Boydell Press.

Campbell, Duncan B. (2003a). *Greek and Roman Artillery 399 BC–AD 363*. Oxford: Osprey Publishing.

Campbell, Duncan B. (2003b) *Greek and Roman Siege Machinery 399 BC–AD 363*. Oxford: Osprey Publishing.

Campbell, Duncan B. (2005a). *Ancient Siege Warfare: Persians, Greeks, Carthaginians and Romans 546–146 BC*. Oxford: Osprey Publishing.

Campbell, Duncan B. (2005b). *Siege Warfare in the Roman World 146 BC–AD 378*. Oxford: Osprey Publishing.

David, Paul K. (2003). *Besieged: 100 Great Sieges from Jericho to Sarajevo*. Oxford: Oxford University Press.

De Vries, Kelly and Robert Douglas Smith (1992). *Medieval Military Technology*. Peterborough, ON: Broadview Press.

Gravett, Christopher (1990). *Medieval Siege Warfare*. Oxford: Osprey Publishing.

Hogg, Ian V. (1975). *Fortress: A History of Military Defence*. London: Purnell & Sons.

Hooper, Nicholas and Matthew Bennett (1996). *Warfare: The Middle Ages 768–1487 (Cambridge Illustrated Atlas)*. Cambridge: Cambridge University Press.

Horrox, Rosemary (1994). *The Black Death*. Manchester: Manchester University Press.

Matheson, Lister M. *Icons of the Middle Ages: Rulers, Writers, Rebels, and Saints*. Westport, CN: Greenwood.

Nicolle, David (2002). *Medieval Siege Weapons (1): Western Europe AD 585–1385*. Oxford: Osprey Publishing.

Nicolle, David (2003). *Medieval Siege Weapons (2): Byzantium, the Islamic World & India AD 476–1526*. Oxford: Osprey Publishing.

Nossov, Konstantin (2003). *Ancient and Medieval Siege Weapons: A Fully Illustrated Guide to Siege Weapons and Tactics*. Staplehurst: Spellmount.

Oman, Sir Charles (1991). *A History of the Art of War in the Middle Ages. Volume 1: 378–1278 AD*. London: Greenhill.

Oman, Sir Charles (1991b). *A History of the Art of War in the Middle Ages. Volume 1: 1278–1485 AD*. London: Greenhill.

Reyerson, Kathryn and Faye Powe, eds (1984). *The Medieval Castle: Romance and Reality*. Dubuque, IA: Kendall/Hunt Publishing Company.

Turnbull, Stephen (2001). *Siege Weapons of the Far East (1) AD 612–1300*. Oxford: Osprey Publishing.

Turnbull, Stephen (2002). *Siege Weapons of the Far East (2) AD 960–1644*. Oxford: Osprey Publishing.

Wiggins, Kenneth (2003). *Siege Mines and Underground Warfare*. Princes Riseborough: Shire.